PRAYER: INTIMACY WITH GOD

BY:

VIRGINIA ECHOLS-HARRISON

First revision of ***Prayer: An Intercourse With God*** – published in 2008 by: Virginia Echols

Prayer: Intimacy With God
Virginia Echols-Harrison, Author

Cover by: Articulate Communications
Produced & Edited by
Articulate Communications
http://www.artcomok.com

Printed in the U.S.A.
© 2008 & 2014

References for all Scripture come from:
THE HOLY BIBLE - KING JAMES VERSION
PARSONS TECHNOLOGY, INC.
Cedar Rapids, Iowa

THE MESSAGE: THE BIBLE IN
CONTEMPORARY LANGUAGE
By: Eugene H. Peterson

QUICKVERSE, A DIVISION OF
FINDEX.COM, INC.
Omaha, Nebraska

No part of this material may be reproduced in any form, other than reasonably short quotes, without the written permission of the author

TABLE OF CONTENTS

Dedication	5
Preface	6
Forward	7
Different Views	14
God's Vulnerability	21
God Seeks Us For Relationship	32
The Human Factor	48
Daily Intimacy/Intercourse A Must	57
Let's Get Married First	73
Approaching The Throne	84
The Essence Of Intimacy/Intercourse	99
Barriers To Empowerment	117
Breaking The Chains	135
Draw Near To God	182
Spiritual "Quickies"	188

Are You Still A "Prayer Virgin?"	196
P.U.Y.S.S.	204
Public Affection	214
The Great Fear	216
The First Love	225
Never Let Him Go	231
Other Books Available	239
Contact Information	241
About The Book	242
About The Author	243

DEDICATION

I dedicate this book to every prayer warrior who has spent the night wrestling with God.

> For thy maker is thine husband (spouse); the LORD of hosts is his name; and thy Redeemer the Holy One of Israel; the God of the whole earth shall He be called. [1]

---

[1] Isaiah 54:5

PREFACE

Christianity is based on a relationship with an individual: that individual is Jesus Christ unlike many other religions.

The very quintessence of relationships is communication. The most intimate relationship in which individuals can engage is the marriage relationship.

As the "bride" of Christ the church is engaged in **spiritual** intimacy with Jesus through prayer, study, and meditation. Hence, *Prayer: Intimacy with God.*

It is the desire of the author that each reader will see that, which God desires for him/her and will in turn yield himself/herself to the control of his/her spiritual husband/spouse - Jesus Christ.

Remember, you can only get to know someone, to the extent that you are willing to be vulnerable to that person; therefore, the more vulnerable you are with that person the more intimate will be the relationship.
Virginia Echols-Harrison, Author

FORWARD

"How beautiful you are, my darling! Oh, how beautiful! Your eyes behind your veil are doves. Your hair is like a flock of goats descending from Mount Gilead. Your teeth are like a flock of sheep just shorn, coming up from the washing. Each has its twin; not one of them is alone. Your lips are like a scarlet ribbon; your mouth is lovely. Your temples behind your veil are like the halves of a pomegranate. Your neck is like the tower of David, built with elegance; on it hang a thousand shields, all of them shields of warriors. Your two breasts are like two fawns, like twin fawns of a gazelle that browse among the lilies. Until the daybreaks and the shadows flee, I will go to the mountain of myrrh and to the hill of incense. All beautiful you are, my darling; there is no flaw in you."[2]

"You have stolen my heart, my sister, my bride; you have stolen my heart with one

---

[2] Song of Solomon 4:1-7 - NIV Bible

glance of your eyes, with one jewel of your necklace. How delightful is your love, my sister, my bride! How much more pleasing is your love than wine, and the fragrance of your perfume than any spice! Your lips drop sweetness as the honeycomb; my bride; milk and honey are under your tongue. The fragrance of your garments is like that of Lebanon. You are a garden locked up, my sister, my bride; you are a spring enclosed, a sealed fountain." [3]

God is the greatest lover ever known to humanity. He possesses the ability to articulate that love in more than a thousand ways. Through the writings of Solomon, we can gather a taste of the way He woos His intended: how he entreats His lover to come and spend time with him. He is not shy in sharing with His darling the things, which pleases Him about His love, His bride. If we were to describe His approach in the colloquial terms of today, we would call him a "smooth talker", for He knows just what to say, to make His sweetheart feel adored.

---
[3] Song of Solomon 4:9-12 - NIV Bible

Although I make no apologies for it, I pray you do not take offence by my bold use of sexual terminology to explain intimacy with God. He makes no apology either. Again, He uses another very daring look at some intimate activity in the book of Ezekiel, chapter 16, where he gives an allegory of unfaithful Jerusalem. He says Jerusalem was born of foreign parents, an Amorite father and a Canaanite mother. Once she was born, they threw her in a field leaving her helpless, still covered with blood. No one wanted her; she was despised. However, one day God came along, before she perished, and commanded her to live.

Therefore, Jerusalem lived and grew up, developed breasts, and became the most beautiful jewel. When she was old enough for love (sex/marriage), he covered her with his garment, which was an indication of his intention to marry her, and he made a covenant of love with her.[4]

---

[4] Ruth 3:8-11

God describes how good he was to Jerusalem, by buying her beautiful clothes, shoes, fine linens and jewelry. He gave her the best food available, treated her like a queen, and her fame spread throughout the earth. However, she was not content with that.

She became vain trusting in her beauty, and became a cheap prostitute. She was so loose that the Scriptures say, "...and hast opened thy feet to everyone that passed by, and multiplied thy whoredoms"... [5] meaning, she would be sexually intimate with whoever passed her way. In her foolishness, she began to give away to her lovers all the wonderful food, jewels and clothing, God had given to her. She sunk so low as to even allow the children she had borne to God to be misused and sacrificed them to her lovers. God called her "weak-willed" and reproved her for being so foolish as to look down on prostitutes who accepted money for their favors; she would not take any money, as if to refuse it would make her

---

[5] Ezekiel 16:25

nobler than a regular whore. Instead, she just gave herself away, along with all that she possessed.

The Lord was utterly disappointed and disgusted with her actions. Moreover, throughout the entire chapter, he goes on and on about her unfaithfulness to him. This chapter and many other Scriptures are replete with examples of God's sexual metaphors toward his people; and He never changes. (Read Ezekiel chapter 16 in MESSAGE Bible for a real shock.)

God calls His church, His bride.[6] He went so far as to have one of his prophets, Hosea, to marry a harlot [7] and have children by her. God did it just so that He could demonstrate to His people, through the hurt and embarrassment of Hosea, the level of pain He experienced whenever Israel allowed others to infringe upon His intimate relationship with them. Additionally, God wanted the Israelites to understand the

---

[6] Isaiah 62:4-5; Revelation 19:7-9
[7] Hosea 1:1-2

correlation between marriage and the covenant of salvation.

Yes, God does not hesitate to talk to His people in overt sexual terminology that they might clearly understand the importance of their affiliation with Him. Again, God is speaking through the pages of this book, concerning the familiarity He desires to share with each of His children today. Will you listen?

> God has revealed Himself, in a limited way, in nature, which gives us glimpses of His power, His wisdom, and His glory. However, nature is unable to reveal clearly God's person, His holiness, His redeeming love, and His everlasting purposes for humankind. Thus, supernatural revelation transcends the "natural" revelation of God in nature, and consists chiefly in God's manifesting

of Himself and His will through **direct intercourse** with humanity.[8]

---

[8] 12 International Standard Bible Encyclopedia (Chicago, IL: The Howard Severance Co., 1915), 3:479, 1480.14

DIFFERENT VIEWS

In the Chinese philosophy, there is a symbol of two inter-twining figures called the Yin and Yang - a spiritual symbol for light and darkness; good and evil; right and wrong; male and female. The dark part of the circle represents negativity and gloom; the white part represents purity and light. The dark part represents the female; the light part represents the male. The dark part represents sickness; the light part represents wellness and health. The two parts co-exist intimately together to bring about harmony and balance between disease and health. Some believe that this is a satanic symbol and represents evil and at some point, it possibly has represented that. However, for the sake of this illustration, if one can bring one's self to broaden his or her spiritual perspective and look a little deeper with the eye of faith, I believe one can gain the ultimate concept of how our lives inter-twine with the God of the universe: Jesus

Christ. I would like to use the positive symbol of the yin and yang as a metaphor, for this book, as it deals with sin and salvation. Please, do not be put off by this; I am not seeking to introduce any "New Age" theology. Hear me out.

In the beginning, there was God: pure and holy, living, in a light that no mere man could approach unto; light which caused angels to veil their faces with their wings.[9] He was (and still is) the Almighty, Omnipresent, Omniscient God, "…with whom is no shadow of turning".[10] Out of love, He created humankind, upright, flawless, and in His own image.[11] Yet despite humanity's beginning, one wrong decision put them **out of harmony** with the creator. Sin entered the world and the **Dis**-ease, the **Dis**-harmony and the **Dis**-respect became paramount.

Adam introduced death to humanity by eating of the fruit, for Scripture says that

---

[9] Isaiah 6:1-3
[10] James 1:17
[11] Genesis 1:26

Eve was deceived, not Adam.[12] After the transgression of Adam, Satan saw that the ruin was complete. The human race reduced to a deplorable condition. Man was now cut-off from **intercourse** with God.[13] Thus, the introduction of **Dis**-ease as illustrated when the two of them hid themselves from God[14] during the cool of the evening, when God came to visit with them. They were no longer *at ease* in his presence, sin formed a wedge between them and God. It would later result in their having to leave their beautiful garden home.

Dis-harmony seeped its way between Adam and Eve, as Adam blamed Eve for the folly of eating the fruit first; then between humankind and beast, as Eve blamed the snake. The pleasant, peaceful existence originally created by God forever destroyed. Male and female, humankind and beast would no longer enjoy the bliss enveloped in

---

[12] I Timothy 2:13-14
[13] Ellen G. White Website – Devotional, **To Have Friends We Must Be Friendly**
[14] Genesis 3:8

the Garden of Eden; one act of **dis**obedience had sent it crashing to the ground.

Lastly, **Dis**-respect was shown toward the creator, himself, when Adam blamed God by saying, "…and **the woman whom thou gavest to be with me**, she gave me of the tree, and I did eat."[15] Adam had the nerve to throw back into God's face, the fact that God had given him the woman: the best of his creation.

One would think that Adam would be eternally grateful to God, and would never have anything negative to say about Eve. For when Adam named all of the animals, he did not find any creature that could have complimented him. So the compassionate God of the universe, desiring to teach mankind a marvelous lesson of **spiritual intimacy**, while at the same time providing companionship for the man, put him to sleep; He removed one of his ribs and with it he built a magnificent, well-constructed, durable and extremely beautiful companion,

---

[15] Genesis 3:12

which would forever bare his title -- wo**man**.[16]

However, Adam failed to admit that he had taken the liberty of willfully eating the fruit himself. He had not been deceived, as Eve had been. He knew better; but sin had already begun its baleful work. However, God knew even more so who the true seducer was. Therefore, in his great love for them, he gave them the promise that one day He would restore them to their Eden home. Jesus (the promised seed) would destroy the snake (devil), and would be man's sacrifice for sin. Then He [17] gently scolded His children, meted out their punishment and sent them out of the garden.

The dark, evil side - Yin - had forced its way into God's creation. God, the father - (Yang) - has ever been unsullied, un-compromised, and unwilling to leave humanity (Yin) in its fallen state. Therefore, laid before the foundation of the world, the

---

[16] Genesis 2:19-23
[17] Genesis 3:15; Ephesians 1:2-8

plan for the rescue of humanity began.[18] God (Yang) would put forth his hand to reunite fallen humanity (Yin) to Himself. The two would solemnly co-exist, bridged together by the sacrifice of Jesus on Calvary. Yin (humanity), fighting the cravings within, yet unable to be freed from the dark, evil, sinful shadow, which binds it, cries out:

> O wretched man that I am! Who shall deliver me from the body of this death? [19]

Then humanity (Yin) feels the presence of Yang (God) beside it; He is comforting, soothing, rescuing and preserving it. Yin cries out loudly once again:

> I thank God through Jesus Christ our Lord. So then with the mind I myself

---

[18] I Peter 1:18-20
[19] Romans 7:24

serve the law of God; but with the flesh the law of sin.[20]

Yang and Yin, God and humanity, perfectly fitted and held together by the saving line of demarcation that separates the colors: Jesus Christ. With Him, there is harmony, balance, wellness and love. Truly, pure open and complete communication can only take place in Jesus until sin has run its course; the world, as we know it ends and God's people eternally saved. Then once again, perfect peace, blessed balance and complete communication will prevail, and we shall be able to intercourse with God face to face, once more.

# # #

---

[20] Romans 7: 25

GOD'S VULNERABILITY

If you will remember, I stated in the preface of this book that you can only get to know someone, to the extent that you are willing to be vulnerable to that person; vulnerably also constitutes humility. It is important that you are willing to humble yourself before another, if you desire to establish true intimacy. Therefore, the more vulnerable you are with that person; the more humble you are the more intimate will be the relationship.

God has not hesitated to make His love and humility known to us from the very beginning of time. One of the greatest texts, found in Scripture, which illustrates His vulnerability is found in the book of John.

> For God so loved the world, that he gave his only begotten Son, that whosoever believeth in him should not perish, but have everlasting

life. For God sent not his Son into the world to condemn the world; but that the world through him might be saved. [21]

What the Apostle John is declaring to us, is that God refused to hold back anything from us, even His only unique Son. The Father was willing to humble Himself and to give Jesus to die for His rebellious created beings that had thumbed their noses in His face and chosen another master. While we were yet sinners, Christ chose to die for us. [22]

The Apostle Paul helps us to understand the fuller effect of John's statement when he announced:

> ...God was in Christ, reconciling the world unto himself, not imputing their trespasses unto them…..…be ye reconciled to God. **For he hath made him *to be* sin for us, who knew no**

---

[21] John 3:16-17
[22] Romans 5:8

sin; that we might be made the righteousness of God in him. [23]

The entire idea regarding Jesus' coming to earth was to lay bare the heart of God to the world; to let humanity see that they had been duped by the enemy of souls and that God was yearning for them to enter into an intimate relationship with Him that could blossom into eternal bliss: to return to their former estate before the fall. Only righteousness/holiness can stand in the presence of God. Therefore, Jesus took on our sin; He took our blame; He was stripped naked and hanged on a cross (His genitalia exposed to all who would look) bearing the shame that was ours; all of this that we might receive His holiness and be drawn into an intimate relationship with Him. He did not mind what the cost might be to Him; He merely wanted to be made one with us, again, no matter the price. Therefore, He gave up all of heaven and the adoration of

---

[23] II Corinthians 5:19-21

angels, was born as one of us that we might be as He.

Truly, God showed His vulnerability and humility toward us, in an effort to develop a saving, loving relationship with us. What will it take for us to get it? How much of himself must He expose before we realize just how much we are loved! Did the stripes on His back from the floggings make a difference to us? Did the nails in His hands and feet, even faze our thinking? What about the weight of sin and the separation from His father's presence? Let us look at just how difficult and painful were those hours that He suffered in Gethsemane, in very intimate prayer with His Father, as described by one of my favorite authors.

> As Christ felt His unity with the Father broken up, He feared that in His human nature He would be unable to endure the coming conflict with the powers of darkness...Everything was at stake with him [Satan]...With the issues of the conflict before Him,

Christ's soul was filled with dread of separation from God. Satan told Him that if He became the surety for a sinful world, the separation would be eternal. He would be identified with Satan's kingdom, and would nevermore be one with God. And what was to be gained by this sacrifice? How hopeless appeared the guilt and ingratitude of men! In its hardest features Satan pressed the situation upon the Redeemer...The people who claim to be above all others in temporal and spiritual advantages have rejected you...One of your own disciples, who has listened to Your instruction, and has been among the foremost in church activities, will betray You. One of Your most zealous followers will deny You. All will forsake You. Christ's whole being abhorred the thought. That those whom He had undertaken to save, those whom He loved so much, should unite in the plots of Satan, this pierced His soul. The conflict was terrible. Its measure was the guilt of His nation, of His accusers and betrayer the guilt of a world lying in wickedness. The sins of men weighed heavily upon Christ, and the sense of God's wrath against sin was crushing out His life...[Yet] from His pale lips comes the bitter cry, 'O My Father, it be possible, let this cup pass from Me.. Nevertheless not as I will, but as Thou wilt.' [24]

In the garden, Jesus was depressed and discouraged. But when the angel came to comfort Him, they left. [25]

When we wrestle with God as Christ did, we will be tempted to fear just as He was.. The enemy will lie to us, as he did to Christ that should we follow God thru straight paths, we will lose credibility with

---

[24] E.G. White, The Desire of Ages, 'Gethsemane' - Chapter 74
[25] E.G. White, Ibid, p 694.1

others; but we must not turn back, just as He refused to turn back.

Vulnerability? Surely, we can easily see it manifested in that garden. I just wonder, how much more vulnerable must we see the Lord, to be convinced that He has first extended Himself toward us to develop this intimate relationship, about which I have been so incessantly writing? What kind of God is this? My, my, my! Well, let me tell you what kind of God He is.

> For thy Maker *is* thine husband; the LORD of hosts *is* his name; and thy Redeemer **the Holy One of Israel**; The God of the whole earth shall he be called. For the LORD hath called thee as a woman forsaken and grieved in spirit, and a wife of youth, when thou wast refused, saith thy God. [26] (Boldness added for emphasis)

He is a Holy God! In addition, He commands us to be holy as well. "...it is

---
[26] Isaiah 54:4-5

written, "be ye holy; for I am holy" I Peter 1:16. Where else is it written to be holy? Leviticus 20:7 - "Sanctify [consecrate] yourselves therefore, and **be ye holy**: for I *am* the LORD your God" (boldness added for emphasis)

Again, God is looking for that unity or oneness of spirit that is to be found and experienced in the marriage relation. He wants that intimate, loving connection between the two of us: an interactive vibrant union. Eugene H. Peterson, author of the Message Bible in Contemporary Language, describes holiness in the following manner:

> Holiness is the most attractive quality, the most intense experience we ever get of sheer life—authentic, firsthand living, not life looked at and enjoyed from a distance. [27]

How are we to understand Mr. Peterson's definition of holiness? I believe

---

[27] E. H. Peterson, Author – Message Bible in Contemporary Language - Introduction to Isaiah

he is saying that our God is genuine; one who can readily be approached and easily interfaced; one with whom we may have a passionate, adoring relationship, unlike any other that we have ever had or ever will have. It is the standard to be reached; it sets the bar! It is something to be sought for, striven for and readily embraced.

In seeking to help us know how awesome the liaison can be on this earth, God describes the relationship, in light of the new earth and how it will be there, for those who will accept it now. Read it closely:

> Regarding Zion, I can't keep my mouth shut, regarding Jerusalem, I can't hold my tongue, Until her righteousness blazes down like the sun and her salvation flames up like a torch. Foreign countries will see your righteousness, and world leaders your glory. You'll get a brand-new name straight from the mouth of God. You'll be a stunning

crown in the palm of God's hand, a jeweled gold cup held high in the hand of your God. No more will anyone call you Rejected, and your country will no more be called Ruined. You'll be called Hephzibah (My Delight), and your land Beulah (Married), Because God delights in you and your land will be like a wedding celebration. For as a young man marries his virgin bride, so your builder marries you, **And as a bridegroom is happy in his bride, so your God is happy with you**. [28] (Boldness added)

Wow! How awesome is that? As a bridegroom is happy in his bride, so your [my] God is happy with you [me]. Don't you want to be as vulnerable to Him as He is toward you? Even now, won't you allow the light of His love to shine into the darkened corners of your heart that you might see the

---

[28] Isaiah 62:1-5 - E. H. Peterson, Author – Message Bible in Contemporary Language

refuse of your sins, which have accumulated and separated Him from the kind of closeness that He craves? He is ready and willing to clean out all of the filthy, damaged areas of your life; and the truth is that He is the only one that can do it! No counselor, no friend, no pastor, no one can do it but Jesus!

Let this Scripture not be true of you:

> And this is the condemnation, that light is come into the world, and men loved darkness rather than light, because their deeds were evil. [29]

He is proposing marriage daily; when will you say, "Yes"? When will you humble yourself to Him that the two of you might be vulnerable to each other? Do it today, only then can you fully experience the joy for which you have longed. He is waiting; do it now.

---

[29] John 3:18

GOD SEEKS US FOR RELATIONSHIP

Let us say, someone offers to build you the house of your dreams, completely furnished with a swimming pool; give you initial $250,000 clothing shopping spree; pre-paid credit cards to cover anything else your heart could desire; your choice of transportation and a lifetime supply of any and all of the food you want. However, there are a few stipulations.

Your house must be built in a remote area away from other people. You must live alone; no one is allowed to visit or interface with you ever, not even your benefactor. As long as you are in possession of any of the items given to you, you must live as a hermit. Nor can you give anything away to anyone.

Question: Would you want to accept the gift? Why or why not?

I'm pretty sure that most of you said, "NO WAY!" None of us would want that gift. Although the accruements sound wonderful, the stipulations leave something to be desired. Why? Because we all know that the greatest joy in having anything, good or bad is to be able to share it with someone else. Relationship is the most important thing God gave us - especially a relationship with Him.

He has always wanted a relationship with us Look at how Isaiah 45:18 describes God's original intent:

> For thus saith the LORD that created the heavens; God himself that formed the earth and made it; he hath established it, he created it not in vain, ***He formed it to be inhabited***: I *am* the LORD; and *there is* none else. (Italics added)

And again, Genesis 1:26 tells us what and how it happened:

> And God said, ***Let us make man in our image, after our likeness***: and let

them have dominion over the fish of the sea, and over the fowl of the air, and over the cattle, and over all the earth, and over every creeping thing that creepeth upon the earth.

However, before God entered into relationship with us; before He formed us in His image, He prepared for our arrival.

And God said, Let there be light: and there was light. And God saw the light, that *it was* good: and God divided the light from the darkness. And God called the light Day, and the darkness he called Night. And the evening and the morning were the first day.

And God said, Let there be a firmament in the midst of the waters, and let it divide the waters from the waters. And God made the firmament, and divided the waters which *were* under the firmament from the waters which *were* above the firmament: and it was so. And God called the firmament Heaven. And the evening and the morning were the second day.

And God said, Let the waters under the heaven be gathered together unto one place, and let the dry *land* appear: and it was so. And God called the dry *land* Earth; and the gathering together of the waters called He Seas: and God saw that *it was* good. And God said, Let the earth bring forth grass, the herb yielding seed, *and* the fruit tree yielding fruit after his kind, whose seed *is* in itself, upon the earth: and it was so. And the earth brought forth grass, *and* herb yielding seed after his kind, and the tree yielding fruit, whose seed *was* in itself, after his kind: and God saw that *it was* good. And the evening and the morning were the third day.

And God said, Let there be lights in the firmament of the heaven to divide the day from the night; and let them be for signs, and for seasons, and for days, and years: And let them be for lights in the firmament of the heaven to give light upon the earth: and it was so. And God made two great lights; the greater light to rule the day, and the lesser light to rule the night: *he made* the stars also. And God set them in the firmament of the heaven to give light upon the earth, And to rule over the day and over the night, and to divide the light from the darkness: and God saw that *it was* good. And the evening and the morning were the fourth day.

And God said, Let the waters bring forth abundantly the moving creature that hath life, and fowl *that* may fly above the earth in the open firmament of heaven. And God created great whales, and every living creature that moveth, which the waters brought forth abundantly, after their kind, and every winged fowl after his kind: and God saw that *it was* good. And God blessed them, saying, Be fruitful, and multiply, and fill the waters in the seas, and let fowl multiply in the earth. And the evening and the morning were the fifth day.

And God said, Let the earth bring forth the living creature after his kind, cattle, and creeping thing, and beast of the earth after his kind: and it was so. And God made the beast of the earth after his kind, and cattle after their kind, and everything that creepeth upon the earth after his kind: and God saw that *it was* good.[30]

God, being the greatest benefactor ever, was keenly aware of what was required for humanity's existence. Therefore, He provided far more than "a house", He gave

---
[30] Genesis 1:1-25 – KJV Bible

us a world, equipped with the finest lighting system; a perfect heating/air conditioning atmosphere; gorgeous landscaping for as far as the eye could see; lush green carpeting; domesticated pets of all shapes, sizes and uniqueness; refreshing oceans and streams of water; pristine air and the melody of heaven. He clothed us in His righteousness, which is far better than the most luxurious earthly wardrobe. Lastly, He crowned His creation with divine and human companionships. [31]

God loves us! He does not wish that we separate ourselves and live in loneliness and despair. He gave us far more than our anonymous benefactor could ever offer, but without those restricting stipulations. The only stipulation He requires is obedience. [32] He wants there to be a threefold unison existent between us: man, woman and God. With this threesome, there will always be relationship, love and success.

---

[31] Genesis 2:18
[32] Genesis 1:16-17

Again, God so loved us that He carved a palace in time just to spend with us; [33] it is called the Sabbath. From the beginning of time, God has longed to be in our presence. The Sabbath, which has always been in existence and which will always be in existence throughout eternity, [34] is designated for us to re-acquaint ourselves with Him. It is a day that is to be filled with prayer, praise, worship and meditation about the greatest friend, lover and savior ever. It is a day designed to remind us of our true creator and of his sustaining power in our lives.

Even after Adam and Eve proved disloyal to Him, God pursued the relationship! Look at the following texts of Scripture:

> And the LORD God said unto the serpent...I will put enmity between thee and the woman, and between thy seed

---

[33] Genesis 2:1-3
[34] Isaiah 66:23

and her seed; it shall bruise thy head, and thou shalt bruise his heel. [35]

God was saying that one day, Christ would be born of a woman; would live, what appeared to be an ordinary life – yet one of perfection. He would do battle with the devil (serpent) and by dying on the cross, would have his heel bruised by him. However, the devil's head would be crushed, when God destroys all of the wicked. Yes, God gave His children/His bride, hope for a renewed relationship, immediately after their severed relationship.

We see examples of God's quest for a relationship with man in the story of the antediluvians and Noah in Genesis 6:8-9:22, as Noah preached and built an ark, only for the people to ignore him. God called Abraham in Genesis 12:1-3, from his idolatrous family who had rejected the God of heaven, to serve Him in a country that He would show him. God re-established the Abrahamic covenant with Isaac in Genesis

---

[35] Genesis 3:14-15

26:1-5. Jacob's name was changed to Israel (overcomer and/or prince with God) as God pursued His servant in Genesis 28:10-15. Again, God intervened for the Israelites, through the story of Joseph in Genesis chapters 37-45; and lastly through Moses in his interaction with the freed slaves in Exodus 3:1-15 and Exodus 19:3 and 16-20.

Sadly, the Children of Israel did not want a relationship with God, as exhibited in Exodus 20:18-19; Numbers 13:32- 14:2, 9-12, 20-24, 26-35. Paul writes:

> Wherefore (as the Holy Ghost saith, To day if ye will hear his voice, Harden not your hearts, as in the provocation, in the day of temptation in the wilderness: When your fathers tempted me, proved me, and saw my works forty years. Wherefore I was grieved with that generation, and said, They do always[s] err in *their* heart; and they have not known my ways. So I sware in my wrath, They shall not enter into my rest.) Take heed, brethren, lest there be in any of you

an evil heart of unbelief, in departing from the living God. But exhort one another daily, while it is called To day; lest any of you be hardened through the deceitfulness of sin. For we are made partakers of Christ, if we hold the beginning of our confidence steadfast unto the end; While it is said, To day if ye will hear his voice, harden not your hearts, as in the provocation. For some, when they had heard, did provoke: howbeit not all that came out of Egypt by Moses. But with whom was he grieved forty years? *was it* not with them that had sinned, whose carcasses fell in the wilderness? And to whom sware he that they should not enter into his rest, but to them that believed not? So we see that they could not enter in because of unbelief. [36]

Their problem doesn't have to be ours. We received this information about them so

---

[36] Hebrews 3:7-19

that we might make better decisions. Jesus bids us today:

> Come unto me, all *ye* that labour and are heavy laden, and I will give you rest. Take my yoke upon you, and learn of me; for I am meek and lowly in heart: and ye shall find rest unto your souls. For my yoke *is* easy, and my burden is light. [37]

Jesus wants us to unite our lives with His life. He wants us to become co-laborers with Him in all of our life's goals. He promises that if we do that, He will carry the weight and will allow us to receive the credit.

Following is another one of my favorite promises. Although originally written to the Israelites upon their entry into Canaan, this is a promise that is still relevant to us today, if we meet the stipulations, which again is merely obedience to what He says.

---

[37] Matt. 11:28-30

But your eyes have seen all the great acts of the LORD which he did...Therefore shall ye keep all the commandments which I command you this day, that ye may be strong, and go in and possess the land, whither ye go to possess it; And that ye may prolong *your* days in the land...the land, whither ye go to possess it, *is* a land of hills and valleys, *and* drinketh water of the rain of heaven: A land which the LORD thy God careth for: the eyes of the LORD thy God *are* always upon it, from the beginning of the year even unto the end of the year.

And it shall come to pass, if ye shall hearken diligently unto my commandments which I command you this day, to love the LORD your God, and to serve him with all your heart and with all your soul, That I will give *you* the rain of your land in his due season, the first rain and the latter rain, that thou mayest gather in thy corn, and thy wine, and thine oil. And I will send grass in thy fields for thy cattle, that thou mayest eat and be full. Take heed to yourselves, that your heart be not deceived, and ye turn aside, and serve other gods, and worship them; And *then* the LORD'S wrath be kindled against you, and he shut up the heaven, that there be no rain, and that the land yield not her fruit; and *lest* ye perish quickly from off the good land which the LORD giveth you.

Therefore, shall ye lay up these my words in your heart and in your soul, and bind them for a sign upon your hand, that they may be as frontlets between your eyes. And ye shall teach them your children, speaking of them when thou sittest in thine house, and when thou walkest by the way, when thou liest down, and when thou risest up. And thou shalt write them upon the door posts of thine house, and upon thy gates: That your days may be multiplied, and the days of your children, in the land which the LORD sware unto your fathers to give them, as the days of heaven upon the earth. [38]

God promises us that if we obey His commandments, teach them to our children and do not serve other gods, then He will in turn answer our prayers, maintain His relationship with us and give us yet greater benefits than originally offered at the creation of the world.

Jesus, our benevolent benefactor says we may have the house of our dreams; [39] our choice of transportation (walk and not be weary, or run and not faint). [40] We can drink from or swim in the river of life that flows from the throne of God and the Lamb. [41]

Our initial shopping spree yields us the priceless robe of Christ's righteousness, again. [42] We have an unlimited supply of our favorite food, which grows monthly from

---

[38] Deuteronomy 11:7-21.
[39] John 14:1-3
[40] Isaiah 40:31
[41] Revelation 22:1
[42] Revelation 19:8

the tree of life. [43] We have a constant stream of everything our hearts could ever desire and it is all pre-paid with the blood of Jesus. Glory hallelujah!

---

[43] Revelation 22:2

THE HUMAN FACTOR

"Nothing is apparently more helpless, yet really more invincible, than the soul that feels its nothingness and relies wholly on the merits of the Saviour. By prayer...by faith in His abiding presence, the weakest of human beings may live in contact with the living Christ and He will hold them by a hand that will never let go." [44]

I experienced no truer words than these when I found myself a captive in my own home; my life threatened.

It was 1970, the summer had been miserable for me as I labored under the weight of childbearing. Sleeplessness and I had become well acquainted. I lay alone in my upstairs bedroom, my two older children peacefully resting across the hall. Halfway beneath my pillow lay the curved leg of an

---

[44] The Ministry of Healing – p. 139, Ellen G. White, Harvestime Books Publisher, Altamont, TN

old dining room table. It was my weapon of defense against any intruder foolish enough to crawl through my broken window at the base of the stairway. It had become my routine to sleep with it ever since my husband and I had parted company.

Suddenly, without warning it was there! The one thing I had dreaded the most – a break-in. The loud thud of the wooden plank falling from the window followed by the scuffling of feet against the outside brick wall alerted me.

Pure adrenaline coursed through my body as I rapidly descended the steps, table leg in hand, headed straight to the window. Deepening my voice as much as I could, trying to sound like a male, I yelled as I brought the table leg hard against the fingers protruding inside of the window, "Get out of here!" I knew I was defenseless against any serious intruder. Here I was three months pregnant, no telephone of any kind in the house to call for help; no weapon other than the one I wielded in my hand and prayer; yes, the precious defense of prayer.

I knew the power of prayer. It had calmed an agitated, depressed mate many nights in this house, as I had talked, sung sweet songs of Zion and rocked him in my arms. On two occasions he was so depressed he talked of suicide. I knew he had a gun, which he kept in the cellar, out of the children's reach. Yet, that was no way to solve his issues; he/we had to rely on God to care for our problems.

It was not until years later that I learned my ex-husband was diagnosed with clinical depression: a condition with which he had suffered from a youth. But who knew? Both of us were clueless as to the extent of the depression that he suffered from time to time, or at least I was. However, I did know that when I prayed and sang to him about God, the bouts of depression would considerably lessen.

Oh, the weapon of prayer! I knew about it and was always armed and ready for battle with the enemy.

"It's me, Billy" I heard a voice call out. "Let me in."

"Let him in?" I wondered to myself. "Why should I let him in? We parted on bad terms, why do I want to let him in?" I mused.

Yet, within my soul I could hear a voice responding to my query; "Let him in" said the voice of the Holy Spirit, and I obeyed.

I stood there, dressed only in my nightgown, the table leg in my hand as he walked through the door.

"What were you planning to do with that?" He chuckled, rubbing his knuckles, as he proceeded to the living room.

"You should know the answer to that" I replied. "I see you rubbing your fingers." We both sat down, he on the couch, me in a stuffed winged back chair.

"So what do you plan to do?" he snarled at me.

"Do about what?" I replied in a similar tone.

"About living here, in this house?"

Before I could reply, the voice of the Holy Spirit spoke to me and said, "A soft answer turns away wrath, but grievous words stir up anger." Then the adrenaline began to subside and a peace washed over my soul. I sat there quietly communing with God, listening for His lead and His direction and I was not disappointed.

The Spirit caused me to realize my utter physical and spiritual helplessness in that situation. In my heart still lay anger and bitterness over our break-up. There was frustration and disappointment regarding our living conditions with seemingly no dignified escape route. The need to forgive, to re-assess, to throw myself upon the mercies of God had not yet been fully embraced. But as I sat there watching my estranged husband, troubled, anxious, desperate for direction, seeking to incite me to anger that he might justifiably complete his mission of homicide/suicide, submission and repentance inundated my soul. God revealed to me that **I had a major part to play in this scenario**. It was vital that I keep still, listen to His voice and immediately obey. God had my attention!

I prayed as never before. Not just for my deliverance but for his deliverance. Moreover, although his thoughts were to physically intimidate and threaten me, God infused me with thoughts to see both of us spiritually delivered and freed from the present circumstances. In what seemed like a lifetime, since he had walked through the door, the answers I did not even know I needed came; heavenly instructions were given and all of my fears subsided.

"Do you hear me talking to you?" he called sarcastically, bringing me back to the moment.

"Yes", I hear you", I replied in a calm and even tone. The Holy Spirit was introducing His presence into the room and permeating my thoughts with His desires. I welcomed Him gladly; the cavalry had arrived. As a result, the conversation proceeded without malice, insinuation or fear, despite the fact that my husband made very clear to me of his homicide/suicide intent.

After about an hour, Billy lay down on the couch, turned his back to me and fell asleep. The enemy of souls called to me and said, "Now is your chance! Hit him in the head; knock him out and get out. It would be considered self-defense." However, the Holy Spirit intruded his conversation and urged me to sit calmly in that chair and just to wait for His instructions. I obeyed.

In every aspect of life, the human factor infiltrates one's decisions. It is important to have a viable relationship with Christ, so that one can more readily make the right choices, through their reliance on Him; for choices must be made and humans must live or die with the result of those choices. God does not relieve us of our part to play in any decision making process. However, He promises that when we reach those crossroads, He would be there, "And thine ears shall hear a word behind thee saying; 'this is the way, walk ye in it, when ye turn to the right hand and when ye turn to the left.'" [45]

---

[45] Isaiah 30:21

The cool night air began to make itself known, as the chill settled upon my bare arms and feet. Yet, I sat still awaiting further instructions. Moreover, once the Spirit let me know that he was asleep, I quickly ascended the steps, gathered a robe and shoes, took my place again in the chair, resting the table leg across my lap, and waited for the morning light. I knew there was nothing that I could accomplish on my own. I had to depend solely, completely, totally on God for the deliverance of my children and me. Only the relationship the Lord and I had formed many years earlier, could sustain me in my hour of trial and tribulation.

> Our only sure defense against besetting sins is prayer, daily and hourly prayer: not one day zealous and the next [day] careless, but through watchfulness and earnestness becoming **vitalized by intercourse with God.**[46]

---

[46] E.G. White - Letter 52, September 25, 1874, to Edson and Emma White.

Although apparently helpless in that situation, I was truly invincible: I felt my nothingness and was relying wholly on the merits of Jesus for liberation. Consequently, by prayer and faith in His abiding presence, I was in contact with the living Christ and He was holding me by a hand that would never let go. Hallelujah!

The next morning, upon hearing my next-door neighbors stirring, I quickly and quietly exited the house; called the police and before nightfall had arranged to move out of the state. I completed my part in the human factor and praised God for His part. It was by prayer, trust and total reliance upon God that I am alive to write about the experience. I have since learned that all God ever wants from us is our trust in Him and our obedience to Him. Everything else will just fall into place.

# # #

DAILY INTERCOURSE IS A MUST

In order to achieve true intimacy, it is important that one develop a sincere relationship. Too many people today are content with superficial relationships that bring no contentment to the heart. This does not have to be so, when it comes to knowing God intimately, you must intercourse with Him daily! The best way that I know to do this is through daily devotion.

In the Old Testament, we read of God's instructions to Israel's priest to conduct morning and evening sacrifices. Let us read it:

> Now this *is that* which thou shalt offer upon the altar; two lambs of the first year **day by day continually**. The **one lamb thou shalt offer in the morning**; and **the other lamb thou shalt offer at even**: And with the one lamb a tenth deal of flour mingled

with the fourth part of an hin of beaten oil; and the fourth part of an hin of wine *for* a drink offering. ⁴¹And the other lamb thou shalt offer at even, and shalt do thereto according to the meat offering of the morning, and according to the drink offering thereof, **for a sweet savor, an offering made by fire unto the LORD.** *This shall be* a continual burnt offering throughout your generations *at* the door of the tabernacle of the congregation before the LORD: where **I will meet you, to speak there unto thee...** [47]

They were to begin and end their day communing or inter-coursing with God. He promised to meet them there and to speak to them. What a fantastic way to begin your day! The God of the entire Universe invites us to meet with Him each day so that He can tell us how to **best** spend it. Then, before we go to bed, He says, "Come and speak or

---

[47] Exodus 29:38-42

intercourse with me again and tell me how you think it went; and if we listen closely, He will tell us whether or not we followed His lead. Awesome! He wants to have continuous passionate intimacy with us! And far too many of us don't even care. However, for those of us who do, we are forever and always in for a treat.

Following are a few pointers that work for me when God and I get together. They have helped me to grow my relationship with God and perhaps they can help you too.

1) I have found that daily devotion builds my love relationship with Jesus. I also believe that the more time you spend with someone, the more you get to know about them. However, if you are not a devoted devotional person, such as me, let me encourage you to begin spending time in devotion much like you would begin an aerobics class. You would not start off in the advanced class where they do continuous moves to fast paced music for at least an hour. You might end-up with a heart attack.

You would first do some warm-ups, followed by stretching then you might engage in roughly 15 minutes of exercise to moderately paced music. Each day you would gradually increase the pace and time until you could keep up with that class. Therefore, try starting out with devotion the same way.

Perhaps you might begin by singing a favorite song and then have opening prayer; select a passage of scripture to read over, perhaps with a commentary for greater understanding. Next, think on what you've read for a few minutes and see how you might apply it to your life. If the Bible cannot be practical to you, then it can be of no value to you. The messages must be applicable in some way to something, somebody or some situation with which you may be involved for you to gain the most from it. Lastly, pray again, only this time lay out before the Lord all of your concerns, prayer requests for others, etc. and ask for His blessings/covering for the day.

2) As you continue to spend time with Jesus, it will help you to understand His truth, and acquaint you with his many wonderful promises. In Jesus' prayer in Gethsemane, He prayed that God would sanctify His followers through the truth. Then He added, "...thy word is truth." [48] Yes, the Word of God is certainly truth and the more you read it, the more sanctifying power it will have over your life. That is what we all need: to be sanctified – set apart for holy use.

One way to do this is to learn a new promise each week, then twice a week eventually working your way up to one each day. It will build your confidence in God, help you to get along better with others and increase your love for them.

3) Daily devotion can help you be an effective witness for Him. Again, the more you learn about Jesus, the more you will want to share what you have learned with others. It is impossible to have an effective relationship with God and not tell anyone. It

---
[48] John 17:3

is like trying to hide a nine-month pregnancy. It just doesn't work! I've found that the greatest and most effective way to witness is to share my personal experiences. No one can refute what is going on with me; it is what I have experienced. Consequently, it keeps me out of arguments with others about faith or religion.

4) Next, spending time with Jesus helps you to successfully combat and defeat the opponent/devil, thus avoiding deception.

> The enemy comes to kill, steal and destroy, said Jesus, but I am come to bring you life and that more abundantly." [49]

Therefore, as you read and apply the following text, you will be prepared to withstand anything.

> Finally, my brethren, be strong in the Lord, and in the power of his might. Put on the whole armour of

---

[49] John 10:10

God that ye may be able to stand against the wiles of the devil. **For we wrestle not against flesh and blood, but against principalities, against powers, against the rulers of the darkness of this world, against spiritual wickedness in high** *places*. Wherefore take unto you the whole armour of God that ye may be able to withstand in the evil day, and having done all, to stand. Stand therefore, having your **loins girt about with truth,** and having on the **breastplate of righteousness**; And your **feet shod with the preparation of the gospel of peace**; Above all, taking the **shield of faith**, wherewith ye shall be able to quench all the fiery darts of the wicked. And take the **helmet of salvation**, and the **sword of the Spirit, which is the word of God: Praying always with all prayer and supplication in the Spirit,** and watching thereunto with all perseverance and supplication for all saints. [50] (bold print added for emphasis)

Paul tells us that we are to get up every day, and dress in battle array. We are to put on every piece of spiritual gear God has provided us. From the head to the feet we are to be covered with the armor of God, in preparation for battle. Nothing is to be left to chance. The place to gather this equipment is at the foot of Jesus in prayer; and through the study of the Holy Bible.

Did you pay attention to the one whom Paul says we are daily doing battle? There is an all-out war going on! When we have conflicts with people, it is not really they who we are in conflict. It is the spirit of evil, with which we are in conflict. Therefore, we don't need to hold grudges against people or dislike them, for they are not the guilty party. It is Jesus' enemy! The wicked one!

In addition, did you notice how Paul mentioned that we should have our "loins"

---

[50] Ephesians 6:10-18,

girt about with truth? Normally, when one thinks of loins, they think about covering the genitalia, however, Peter makes clear what Paul is trying to say in I Peter 1:13-16:

Wherefore gird up the **loins of your mind**, be sober, and hope to the end for the grace that is to be brought unto you at the revelation of Jesus Christ; As **obedient children, not fashioning yourselves according to the former lusts in your ignorance**: But as he which hath called you is holy, so be ye holy in all manner of conversation; Because it is written, Be ye holy; for I am holy. (bold print added for emphasis)

Peter is explaining what Paul meant by loins; it has to do with the mind, the thinking, the forefront (frontal lobe) of your brain where all the decisions are made. Whatever action you take in any direction has first been settled or decided upon in your mind. That is why "truth" is so important. If you know the "truth" about an issue, you can make better decisions, for you can weigh the outcome on both sides. This is a serious matter, which is why daily devotion, with Him who is "Truth"[51] is so very vital. It's important that we connect with Him daily.

The Apostle Paul also admonishes us, to:

> Let this mind be in you, which was also in Christ Jesus: Who, being in the form of God, thought it not robbery to be equal with God: But made himself of no reputation, and took upon him the form of a servant, and was made in the likeness of men: And being found in fashion as a man, he humbled himself, and became obedient unto death, even the death of the cross... [52]

Although Jesus is God, He was willing to humble himself, avoiding calling attention to himself, but promoting His Father's will and even allowing Himself to

---

[51] John 14:6
[52] Philippians 2:5-8

be killed on Calvary. This is the kind of mind we need - a humble, willing, obedient mind. You can develop one through daily devotion/spending time with Jesus.

5) This is how you build-up your spiritual muscles, which are necessary for combat. If you are in training for any physical activity, it is necessary to put forth your all, building up muscles, increasing your endurance and developing the right attitude for victory. Daily devotion does this for you. The more you exercise your spiritual muscles of prayer and Bible study, the stronger and more resolute you'll become; and the odds of your being able to stand through the last great trial that is coming upon the world, will be increased greatly.

6) Daily devotion with Jesus helps to intensify your desire for heaven, and to discard the things of this world. If all you do is eat sweets all of the time, you will lose your appetite for plain food. The same stands true for spending all of your free time watching television, playing games, talking

about the latest movie or movie star. If this is all that you allow your mind to feed upon, then soon you will lose the desire to read your Bible, attend religious services or pray; and when you do engage in them, they will hold very little interest for you. It is very important that you feed your spiritual appetite or you will spiritually die. We are told:

> But we all, with open face beholding as in a glass the glory of the Lord, are changed into the same image from glory to glory, *even* as by the Spirit of the Lord. [53]

This same principle applies if we behold evil. If we behold good, then we will be positively transformed. If we behold evil, then we will be negatively transformed. The choice is yours.

7) Lastly, by engaging in daily devotion with Jesus, you receive insight into the role God intends for you to play in his

---

[53] II Corinthians 3:18

kingdom. In the book of James, John and Matthew and we pick up these marvelous promises.

> If any of you lack wisdom, let him **ask of God**, that giveth to all *men* liberally, and upbraideth not; and it shall be given him. But let him ask in faith, nothing wavering [54] (bold print added for emphasis)

> ...My doctrine is not mine, but his that sent me. **If any man will do his will, he shall know of the doctrine**, whether it be of God, or *whether* I speak of myself [55] (bold print added for emphasis)

> No man can serve two masters: for either he will hate the one, and love the other; or else he will hold to the one, and despise the other. Ye cannot serve God and mammon.

---
[54] James 1:5-6
[55] John 7:16-17

Therefore I say unto you, Take no thought for your life, what ye shall eat, or what ye shall drink; nor yet for your body, what ye shall put on. Is not the life more than meat, and the body than raiment? Behold the fowls of the air: for they sow not, neither do they reap, nor gather into barns; yet your heavenly Father feedeth them. Are ye not much better than they? Which of you by taking thought can add one cubit unto his stature? And why take ye thought for raiment? Consider the lilies of the field, how they grow; they toil not, neither do they spin: And yet I say unto you, That even Solomon in all his glory was not arrayed like one of these. Wherefore, if God so clothe the grass of the field, which today is, and tomorrow is cast into the oven, *shall he* not much more *clothe* you, O ye of little faith? Therefore take no thought, saying, What shall we eat? or, What shall we drink? or, Wherewithal shall we be clothed? (For after all these things do the Gentiles seek:) for your heavenly Father knoweth that ye have need of all these things. **But seek ye first the kingdom of God, and his righteousness; and all these things shall be added unto you.** [56] (bold print added for emphasis)

If you want to know God's will for your life, just ask Him, seek after Him, be willing to obey Him and He will answer. He is more than willing, not only to tell you, but to lead you every step of the way. All you need to do is give Him permission to lead you into the paths He would have you to go.

In closing, the best choice you can make in life is to spend time with Jesus every day. Remember, it is all preparation for heaven. If you find it difficult to spend time with Him on earth, you will not make it to heaven for you would be most unhappy and Jesus does not want you to be unhappy. He loves you enough to respect whatever

---

[56] Matthew 6:25-33

choice you make. There are only two of them: heaven or hell. Choose wisely.

#

LET'S GET MARRIED FIRST

We have discovered that relationship is very important to God. Nevertheless, in order to have intimacy with Him, you must marry Him. If you will not consent to marriage, He will not consent to relations with you. He is not an adulterer or a fornicator, and as such, does not encourage either. Therefore, since we are talking about prayer as a form of intimacy (intercourse) with God, then we must conclude that God only hears the prayers of those to whom He is married -- namely His bride -- the church. "But", I can hear you saying now "God will hear sinners when they pray, otherwise, they could never be saved." To this statement, comes a very logical answer.

When, as a sinner, you earnestly call upon God to answer a prayer, you accept God's request for your hand in marriage. You see, God proposes,

> And I will betroth thee unto me forever, yea, I will betroth thee unto me in righteousness, and in judgment, and in loving kindness, and in mercies. I will even betroth thee unto me in faithfulness: and thou shall know the LORD. [57]

In your plea to God to intervene in any given condition (e.g. to save you from disaster, to open a door of opportunity, to heal a child, etc.) you enter a contractual agreement with God by admitting your own helplessness in the situation, and by relying upon his power, to effect a change. Thus, the foundational proposal to enter a long-term relationship has been established. Your status toward God has changed. No longer are you a rebellious, stiff-necked individual, but a willing suppliant of the Father's kingdom. Hence, you become, at that moment, the bride of Christ.

As His bride, will you always be faithful to Him? There is a strong possibility

---
[57] Hosea 2:19-20

that you will not be. However, the act of initially yielding your will to His is equivalent to "jumping the broom" or engaging in the marriage ceremony. In addition, although you may go on to play the harlot like Israel; God will plead with you, for a while, as He pled with Israel. "Turn, O backsliding children, saith the Lord; for **I am married** unto you:"[58]

Again, He says,

> THEY SAY, 'If a man put away his wife, and she go from him, and become another man's, shall he return unto her again?' Shall not that land be greatly polluted? But thou hast played the harlot with many lovers; yet return again to me, saith the LORD. [59]

In His love and dedication to His church, He further promises,

---

[58] Jeremiah 3:14
[59] Jeremiah 3: 1

But if the wicked will turn from all his sins that he hath committed, and keep all my statues, and do that which is lawful and right, he shall surely live, he shall not die. All his transgressions that he hath committed, they shall not be mentioned unto him: in his righteousness that he hath done he shall live. Have I any pleasure at all that the wicked should die? Saith the Lord GOD: and not that he should return from his ways, and live? [60]

When you marry Christ, He wants you to be lovingly obedient, willing to abide by the rules of his household. Daily, there must be a yielding of your will to His will, if the marriage is to work. Failure on your part to surrender, at any given time, constitutes adultery. He commands you to keep his laws. However, He promises to help you. The marriage contract promises:

---

[60] Ezekiel 18:21-23

A new heart also will I give you, and a new spirit will I put within you: and I will take away the stony heart out of your flesh, and I will give you a heart of flesh. And I will put my spirit within you, and cause you to walk in my statutes, and ye shall keep my judgments, and do them.[61]

Therefore, when you come to God for help, God immediately responds and justifies you from all former sins. [62] No longer are you outsiders, cumbered with the weight of sin, but you immediately become the bride of Christ. Thus, the honeymoon begins. Moreover, God, our Father, by His example of loving humanity first,[63] teaches you to love Him and his law.

The Apostle John says, "For this is the love of God, that we keep His commandments: and His commandments are not grievous." [64] "Why?" you ask? Well

---

[61] Ezekiel 36:26-27
[62] Romans 3:24-25
[63] I John 4:10 & 4:19
[64] I John 5:3

when God talks about commandments, He is also talking about law. "In the Hebrew language the term "torah" (law) comes from the word 'horah', meaning 'to point out,' 'to teach,' or 'to instruct' ... in the broadest sense 'teaching' or instruction.'...In this sense the word law signifies *all the revealed will of God, or any part of it.*"[65]

In the book of Deuteronomy [66] you read:

> And now, Israel, what doth the LORD thy God require of thee, but to fear the LORD thy God, to walk in all His ways, and to love Him, and to serve the LORD thy God with all thy heart and with all they soul, to keep the commandments of the LORD, and His statues, which I *command* thee this day *for thy good?*

---

[65] The Promise, 1st Quarter S.D.A (Teacher's Ed.) - Pacific Press, Nampa, ID [93] (Italics supplied for emphasis)
[66] Deuteronomy 10:12-3

This concept of obedience is also much like being a parent. As parents, we command the best from our children. We teach them social graces (e.g. "'Please", "Thank you" and "May I?"). We teach them health principles (e.g. bathing, brushing and grooming). We teach them spiritual applications (e.g. praying, praising and meditating). All of these things and more, we purposely teach our children, and expect them to practice and/or abide by these rules. In many instances, they "fall short" (e.g. fight, spit on others, fail to bathe, exercise proper manners, etc.) and we reprimand them. The same principles apply to us, relative to God our Father, as do the principles we apply toward our children. We demand compliance for their best good, knowing that if they are obedient, their lives will be happier, and so will everyone else who interfaces with them. God knows if we comply and are obedient to his laws and commandments, the same will be true for us.

I remember when I was a child, my mother used to say to me, "I'm trying to raise you, so that someone will love you other than me." That saying completely puzzled me until I had my own children, and realized the importance of teaching them obedience and good manners. No one wants to be around an unruly, ill-tempered child. Teachers do not want to teach them and children do not want to play with them. Ostracized, these children feel abandoned. Many will act out just to get attention or to feel as though they are a part of the group. Moreover, others will join a "street gang", so that they can feel a part. However, the saddest aspect of it all is that those children will be unhappy children, simply because they failed to learn obedience.

As the bride of Christ, we must, just as He did when upon the earth, abide by His Father's laws/rules/commandments, so that we, too, can be happy and protected. For as long as we stay within the parameters of His law, we are safe from the law.

God is a just and merciful God, who does not fail of blessing sinners, whether or not they realize or even acknowledge the blessing. The record states,

> For he maketh his sun to rise on the evil and on the good, and sendeth rain on the just and on the unjust."[67]

God does not withhold his kindness to sinners, but rather through this kindness, He seeks to draw the reprobate to Himself. He wants the offender to see and understand His mercy and His grace, so that the sinner might realize that God is open and approachable. No one would ever come to Him, if it were not for the fact that God first reveals himself to humankind by favor and long-suffering then invites him or her through His love.

However, God will not abide a backsliding wife forever. If you fail to repent and follow Him, after He repeatedly forgives you, He says, "He will divorce

---

[67] Matthew 5:45

you", [68] and you will become worse than you were from the beginning.

> For it had been better for them not to have known the way of righteousness, than, after they have known it, to turn from the holy commandment delivered unto them. But it is happened unto them according to the true proverb, 'the dog is turned to his own vomit again; and the sow that was washed to her wallowing in the mire'. [69]

Therefore, when you pray to God, you come as a sinner in need of salvation, on some level. You may not realize your total need of salvation from sin at that time, but you realize that you are faced with a problem, which needs a power greater than yourself. Therefore, as soon as you humble yourself before God, acknowledging His power to manage the situation, marriage and

---

[68] Jeremiah 3:8
[69] II Peter 2:21-22

intimacy between you and Christ takes place. Hence, adultery never enters the picture. The converted you become the legalized bride of Christ.

###

APPROACHING THE THRONE

Shared in the Old Testament, is a thought-provoking story in the book of Esther. In fact, the entire book is about her, her people, her eventful choice to be crowned queen and her reign.

When you consider Esther, as Queen of Persia, you come to realize that she held the second most powerful position in the **world**; for Mede-Persia was the second world-wide nation and Persia had emerged over the Median section, thereby becoming prominent. Her presence commanded obeisance, her wishes brought instant gratification, and her beauty was a delight and a pleasure to behold. When she spoke, servants, statesmen and ambassadors obeyed. In addition, her voice and choice were laden with authority. She entertained local dignitaries and doubtless noble personages of other countries. Her favors and influence were sought after, and her status envied by every single maiden in the land. Yet with all of this pomp, prestige and power, she was still subject to her husband, the king, and the richest of all the previous Persian kings.

The story reads that [70] Mordecai, Esther's cousin, was very distraught over the fact that Haman, a Jewish adversary, had petitioned the king to kill all of the Jews. Because of his hatred for Mordecai, he offered the king a huge sum of money, if the king would allow him to destroy these people and thus he would rid himself of Mordecai and anymore like him, because Mordecai refused to bow to him. Haman accused the Jews, to the king of having their own laws, and therefore did not obey the laws of Persia. His argument was totally unfounded, yet with the offer to pay 10,000 talents of silver, (which equates to millions of dollars in our day) into the treasury, the king agreed. King Ahasuerus did not know, however, that Esther was a Jew also, when he consented to the destruction of this group

---

[70] Esther 4:1 - 5:14

of people. Notices went to all of the provinces, announcing that on a certain day, all the Jews were to be killed and their possessions would go to the men who killed them.

Mordecai was, understandably, very upset with hearing this news and put on sackcloth and sat, by the king's gate, in ashes (something the Jewish people did to show sadness and/or remorse). When Esther learned of Mordecai's actions (not knowing about the decree), she sent him new clothes to cheer him up, but he refused them. Instead, he sent a message back to Esther to intervene, with the king, on behalf of the Jewish people to spare their lives. At first Esther refused, but upon receiving a scathing rebuke from Mordecai saying,

> Think not with thyself that thou shalt escape in the king's house, more than all the Jews. For if thou altogether holdest thy peace at this time, then shall there enlargement and deliverance arise to the Jews from

another place; but thou and thy father's house shall be destroyed: and who knowest whether thou art come to the kingdom for such a time as this? [71]

Esther had refused, not because she was unsympathetic, but because she knew, the Persian law stated:

> …whosoever, whether man or woman, shall come unto the king into the inner court, **who is not called**, there is one law of his to put him to death, except such to whom the king shall hold out the golden scepter, that he may live:.. [72]

Evidently, the king had been too busy with his duties and/or his concubines, to call Esther to his chamber (30 days had passed since the king had called for her). Thus, she feared that if she went in unto him

---

[71] Esther 4:13-14
[72] Esther 4:11

uninvited, she would die. However, after hearing from her cousin, who had raised her from a child after the death of her parents, she prepared to approach the king's throne.

Esther took the idea of approaching the king's throne very seriously. Despite the fact that she was the queen, and by her position alone, she could cause the hearts of her subjects to quake in fear; she now quaked with that same fear, at the thought of going, uninvited, into the king's presence. Therefore, she made careful preparation, for this inconceivable step.

> If the Spirit beareth witness with our spirit that we are the children of God, what is the result? The believing soul comes into perfect submission to the will of God. **The Majesty of heaven condescends to a holy, familiar <u>intercourse</u> with him who seeks God with the whole heart, and the child of God, through the abundant manifestation of His grace, is softened into a childlike de-**

pendence. You must commit your soul and body unto God with perfect trust in His power and willingness to bless you, helpless and unworthy as you are.[73]

Therefore, she began her preparation by first sending orders to Mordecai and all the provinces of the Jews to fast for three days. Can you imagine millions of people, voluntarily, not eating for that long? Next, she ceased to eat, and commanded her immediate servants to do the same during that time. For a full three days and nights, no one would eat nor drink preceding her contact with the king. You see Esther understood this concept,

> ...Cursed be the man that trusteth in man, and maketh flesh his arm, and whose heart departeth from the LORD... Blessed is the man that trusteth in the LORD, and whose hope the LORD is. For he shall be as a tree

---

[73] E.G. White Website - 14MR 276.2

planted by the waters, and that spreadeth out her roots by the river, and shall not see when heat cometh, but her leaf shall be green; and shall not be careful in the year of drought; neither shall cease from yielding fruit."[74]

Following that concept, she sent a message to Mordecai "…and so will I go in unto the king, which is not according to the law: and if I perish, I perish.[75]

Then, when the day arrived, she put on her "royal apparel" [76] went and stood in the inner court of the king's house.

I imagine during those three days of fasting and prayer, there was very little sleeping going on, because a certain kind of mind-set needed to be developed. There was too much at stake to risk beclouding the senses with food. All of the blood, which

---

[74] Jeremiah 17:5,7-9
[75] ibid 4:16
[76] ibid 5:1

would drain from the brain and go to the stomach, to help digest any physical intakes, must be reserved to battle with the fears and trepidations that sought to overcome their souls. Therefore, when the day finally arrived for her to take that walk, she no doubt did it with an air of confidence and resolution. She was intrepid as she took her place in the king's inner court, and waited for his response. Would he extend the scepter? On the other hand, would she die?

Approaching the throne of God is a more fearful act, than the one taken by Esther. Despite the fact that you are the king's bride, for He has "betrothed you unto himself", [77] you are still subject to his authority. You cannot approach the throne of God and act as if He is a peon, like you, with no ability to effect the decisions of the world, or change the outcome for any of His discontentments. He is not your "homeboy" or your "dawg" although his ear is ever open to your cries, and He will gladly entertain your presence. He is not your subordinate, to

---
[77] Hosea 2:19

whom you can give orders and expect fulfillment, as you have dictated. Although he promises

> And this is the confidence that we have in Him, that, if we ask any thing according to His will, He heareth us; and if we know that He hear us, whatsoever we ask, we know that we have the petitions that we desired of him. [78]

You must remember that **HE IS THE KING OF THE UNIVERSE!** You must be mindful and respectful when approaching His throne.

In order to approach the throne of God, and not meet with displeasure, you need to have the right mind-set, like Esther. She knew she just could not go walking into the king's chamber as if she owned it, or with any air of insolence. She realized she had to humble her mind and heart. She needed to put things in their right

---

[78] I John 5:14-15

perspective. Even though she had power because of her affiliation with him, she realized that it was only her affiliation with him that gave her power! Therefore, she needed to approach his throne in meekness and with fear. When it comes to God, so should you.

The Scripture says, you are to "Fear God, and keep his commandments..."[79] "Fear God, for the hour of His judgment is come..." [80] That fear can be interpreted as *grave respect*. When you approach the throne of God, it should be with a self-effacing respect for whom and what He is: *The Omnipresent God, Creator of the Universe*. In order to develop this appropriate state of mind, fasting may very well be what is needed that you may see and appreciate Him better. Do not dare to assume the attitude that because you are His bride, a member in good standing in the church, or an officer in his vineyard that you have any power! You can have no power

---

[79] Ecclesiastes 12:13
[80] Revelation 14:7

except that, which God gives to you. Listen to how Jeremiah describes it,

> Fear ye not me? Saith the LORD: will ye not tremble at my presence, which have placed the sand for the bound of the sea by a perpetual decree, that it cannot pass it: and though the waves thereof toss themselves, yet can they not prevail; though they roar, yet can they not pass over it? [81]

> Thus saith the LORD, let not the wise man glory in his wisdom, neither let the mighty man glory in his might, let not the rich man glory in his riches: But let him that glorieth glory in this, that he understandeth and knowest me, that I am the LORD which exercise loving kindness, judgment, and righteousness, in the earth; for in these things I delight, saith the LORD. [82]

---
[81] Jeremiah 5:22
[82] Jeremiah 9:23-24

Next, as you approach His throne, you need to put on your "royal apparel", which is the righteousness of Christ-- "...and this is the name wherewith He shall be called, The LORD our Righteousness". [83] When you approach the throne of God, it should be in the name of Jesus. Only His merits are recognized in the throne room of God. Jesus said that shortly before his crucifixion.

> And whatsoever ye shall ask in my name, that will I do, that the Father may be glorified in the Son. If ye shall ask anything in my name, I will do it. [84]
>
> Hence, "...The work of righteousness shall be peace; and the effect of righteousness quietness and assurance forever." [85]

Consequently, when you acquire the correct attitude; when you humble yourself

---

[83] Jeremiah 33:16
[84] St. John 14:13-14
[85] Isaiah 32:17

before the Lord your maker; when you fear sinning against God and totally respect His power and authority; when you adorn yourself with the righteousness of Christ, which is an obedient, believing spirit, then, and only then can you approach the throne of God **with assurance**. Then and only then, can you "...Come boldly unto the throne of grace, that we (*you*) may obtain mercy, and find grace to help in time of need." [86]

When you have met these requirements, then like Esther, you may approach the throne without trepidation, assured that the scepter of His grace, coupled with mercy, will be held out to you; and you will live.

The door to his inner court is always open, and he bids you:

> Come unto me, all ye that labour and are heavy laden and I will give you rest. Take my yoke upon you, and learn of me; for I am meek and lowly

---

[86] Hebrews 4:16 (*you* is added for emphasis)

in heart: and ye shall find rest unto your soul. [87]

Again, he says:

Look unto Me, and be ye saved, all the ends of the earth: for I Am God, and there is none else. I have sworn by Myself, the word is gone out of My mouth in righteousness, and shall not return. That unto Me every knee shall bow, every tongue shall swear. Surely, shall one say, in the LORD have I righteousness and strength: even to Him shall men come; and all that are incensed against Him shall be ashamed. In the LORD shall all the seed of Israel be justified, and shall glory.[88]

Daily, the Lord is extending His scepter to you; He wants you to come and intercourse with Him. If you do, I guarantee

---

[87] Matthew 11:28-29
[88] Isaiah 45:22-25

you, your burdens will slip away from your shoulders as easily as a leather purse strap slips from a satin blouse. Your stress will dissipate and your joy will be full, at the throne of God.

#

THE ESENCE OF INTIMACY/INTERCOURSE

If you have not read the preceding chapters, please stop now and do so. Failure to read them will give you a skewed understanding about this chapter and will cause you to fail of receiving its full benefit. Thank you.

I needed a topic for a prayer breakfast, something with teeth in it. A topic, which would cause every attendee present, to be glad he/she came; something beyond the mundane of Hebrews 11:6 ("He that cometh to God, must believe that he is, and that he is a rewarder of them which diligently seek him."), which is quoted repeatedly at so many prayer breakfasts I've attended. It is not that that is a bad Scripture, no Scripture is bad; but hearing it repeated at every session of this nature can make it appear mundane. I wanted the audience to sit-up and pay attention, not just wave off the message as I had seen them do others, on too many occasions. Consequently, on the Tuesday preceding the affair, as I stood in my shower, the warm water pulsating over my shoulders, I earnestly began to pray.

In addition to the prayer engagement, scheduled for that upcoming Sabbath morning was a preaching engagement, for youth day, at a church in Oklahoma City followed by a workshop in the afternoon. With having to speak on two separate topics on the same day, I had been wrestling with the themes, and asking God to lead me to the right Scriptures, as well as the most appropriate approaches. However, the one engagement that engrossed my thoughts presently was the prayer breakfast. I did not seem to be able to pull my thoughts away from it. I was excited about this speaking appointment. Having started a prayer band at my church, with other women in my age group, had brought me hours of encouragement and satisfaction; and I looked forward to sharing with those women on Sunday morning some of the wonderful blessings, which had come to us as a result.

Therefore, I showered and prayed that the Lord would help me to keep my thoughts clearly focused on each presentation. I knew He would use me, for I was open to His bidding, and that is essentially all that He requires of us.

Suddenly, my mind seemed charged, from an outside force. Thoughts of how God looks at us, of His great love toward us and how He wishes to spend time with us engulfed my view. The thought pressed my conscientiousness that *prayer is intimacy or intercourse with God.* It is not just the verbal exchange that so many have grown accustomed to -- that of giving God a list of things they need or want done and then waiting to see what will happen -- but a living, vibrant, exciting, satisfying occurrence, which is better when experienced than when discussed.

It did not dawn on me at the time, but the following quote had to have been in my subconscious, for I had read the book from which it came at least a dozen times. This is what the quote says:

Through nature and revelation, through His providence, and by the influence of His Spirit, God speaks to us. But these are not enough; we need also to pour out our hearts to Him. In order to have spiritual life and energy, **we must have actual intercourse** with our heavenly Father. Our minds may be drawn out toward Him; we may meditate upon His works, His mercies, His blessings; but this is not, in the fullest sense, communing with Him. In order to commune with God, we must have something to say to Him concerning our actual life.[89]

I have heard some people refer to prayer as pouring out one's soul to God. Others say it is communion with God. One of my favorite authors says:

Prayer is the opening of the heart to God as to a friend. Not that it is

---

[89] E.G. White – Steps to Christ - The Privilege of Prayer, Chap.11

necessary in order to make known to God what we are, but in order to enable us to receive Him. Prayer does not bring God down to us, but brings us up to Him.[90]

Moreover, the thought that was impressed upon my mind that afternoon, was that prayer is like making love with one's spouse, only better – **it is intercourse.** But wait! Before you die of exasperation at the concept, keep reading; you will gain a delightfully new concept about God that will increase your relationship with Him fourfold. Therefore, the question is, "What exactly is intercourse?"

In Genesis 4:1 we read, "Now Adam *knew* Eve his wife, and she conceived and bore Cain…" The word 'knew' comes from the Hebrew root word, yada', pronounced ya-dah'. [91] Defined as: 1) to know by

---

[90] Steps to Christ – 'The Privilege of Prayer' p. 93 - Ellen G. White, Review & Herald, Washington, D.C.
[91] "Hebrew Lexicon :: H3045 (KJV)." Blue Letter Bible. Sowing Circle. Web. 24 Mar, 2014.

experience; 2) to know a person carnally; and 3) to know or be acquainted with. This same word is also used in the following texts of Scripture.

> A. Before I formed thee in the belly I *knew* thee; and before thou camest forth out of the womb I sanctified thee, and I ordained thee a prophet unto the nations. Jeremiah 1:5

> B. And then will I profess unto them, I never *knew* you: depart from me, ye that work iniquity. Matthew 7:23

> C. Because that, when they *knew* God, they glorified him not as God, neither were thankful; but became vain in their imaginations, and their foolish heart was darkened. Romans 1:21

> D. Behold, what manner of love the Father hath bestowed upon us, that we

---

<http://www.blueletterbible.org/lang/lexicon/lexicon.cfm?Strongs=H3045&t=KJV>.

should be called the sons of God: therefore the world knoweth us not, because it ***knew*** him not.   1 John 3:1

All of these references to the word "knew" indicate an intimacy with another being, (i.e. intercourse).

As defined by the Encarta Dictionary; English (North America) intercourse is: (1) Same as sexual intercourse; (2) Mutual dealings – exchanges between people or groups, **especially conversation** or social activity. [92]

The essence: the very kernel and heart of prayer is **intercourse! Intimacy! Conversation!** God encourages us, when we come in prayer, to be specific in our requests, to make our needs known unto Him. Think about it! It is intercourse on a higher holier level. It is the most intimate exchange of communication a person can have with another. It is the "baring of the soul to another," revealing the good and the bad.

---

[92] Encarta Dictionary; English (North America)

When you pray to God, you consciously expose your vulnerability to Him like at no other time. Your soul is stripped of its self-righteousness; you stand naked before your maker, unable to hide any of your faults or defects. Your dimples of doubt, your love handles of iniquity are fully exposed; yet you can be comfortable with it, because you know He will not hurt you; take unfair advantage of you, make fun of you, belittle you, or just use you and toss you aside. He has your greatest interest at heart. He understands your self-consciousness, and He longs to put you *at ease*: the yin-yang theory kicks in. So he bids you, "...when thou prayest, enter into thy closet, and when thou hast shut thy door, pray to thy Father which is in secret; and thy Father which seeth in secret shall reward thee openly."[93] No one else needs to see you in the "spiritual" buff, just God!

When you desire to be with Him, to really be with Him in totality, then go into your closet - into a private place - and shut

---

[93] Matthew 6:6

the door, because something exciting is about to happen. You do not want any nosey neighbors, disturbing distractions, or ringing telephones to disturb the mood, or to interfere with you being with your lover, Jesus Christ. Something intimate and holy is going to take place with some possible moaning and groaning going on (with the Holy Spirit translating those things, which cannot be uttered).[94] You need your privacy to cry aloud, to shout His name, even to call Him Abba (daddy), if you choose. It is a private affair, so you can relax and enjoy His presence.

Being with God alone is both relaxing and invigorating; it is stimulating and sedating; it is joyful yet you sometimes cry. It is confrontational yet conciliatory; it is reproving yet rewarding; it is intimidating yet intimately enticing. It is an overwhelmingly audacious adventure!

Yes, being alone with God, in prayer, is incredible! You can experience the awareness anytime of day or night. Seeking

---

[94] Romans 8:26

satisfaction, whenever you feel the need, He is always ready and available. There is never any excuse given as to why you must wait or suffer frustration. Nor is there any unnecessary pressure placed upon you to enter His chamber, if you do not wish to be there. However, the door is always open and satisfaction guaranteed, if you come with the right attitude and stay long enough.

Human lovemaking is to be a holistic experience and although your human mate may not always understand that concept, God certainly does. That is why he woos your mind and draws you into an intellectual exchange with himself. (*"Come now and let us reason together, saith the Lord..."*[95]), before you experience any type of release from your cares and woes of the world. Hear Him as He says, "... *Yea, I have loved thee with an everlasting love: therefore, with loving-kindness have I drawn thee*". [96]

He knows that when two people first come together, each of them is tentative

---

[95] Isaiah 1:18
[96] Jeremiah 31:3

about making a commitment; therefore, He puts Himself on the line - "...he first loves us (you)..."[97] "He is love." [98]

He assures you that He will not hurt you, by saying, "There is no fear in love. But perfect love drives out fear ..."[99]

He reminds you of the many titles He has conferred upon you:

> How great is the love the Father has lavished on us (*you*) that we (you) should be called *children of God*! ... [100]

Oft times, you may think about the many lovers your mate could have chosen. Sometimes you may be tempted to wonder just why your mate selected you over so many others perhaps more beautiful, more handsome, more intelligent or more successful than yourself. But God gives you the assurance about His choice:

---

[97] I John 4:19 NIV
[98] I John 4:10 NIV
[99] I John 4:18
[100] I John 3:1 NIV; St. John 1:12

> The Lord did not set his affection on you and choose you because you were *more*[101] numerous than other peoples, for you were the fewest of all peoples. *But it was because the Lord loved you…*[102]

Truly, He wants you to know how special you are to Him; He wants to ravish your mind with intimate thoughts about how you turn Him on, and how you stand out from all the rest. With Him, you are not a second thought, but rather the first, for He was making plans for you to be with Him, from the very beginning; [103] "…he ever liveth to make intercession for them (you)."[104]

Have you ever fretted that your mate will leave you for someone else? Alternatively, that he/she will one day fall out of love with you? Maybe you are concerned that hard times will drive the two of you far apart from each other. These are legitimate

---
[101] Italics supplied
[102] Deuteronomy 7:7-8 NIV
[103] Matthew 25:34
[104] Hebrews 7:25

concerns, considering how great the divorce rate is today. However, God says, "*I will never leave thee, nor forsake thee*". [105] Again, He commits to saying,

> ...Neither death, nor life, nor angels, nor principalities, nor powers, nor things present, nor things to come, nor height, nor depth, nor any other creature, *shall be able to separate us (you)*[106] from the love of God ... [107]

This brings me to another point. I am the youngest of nine children - four sisters and five brothers - and the smallest of them all. I grew up in a little town - less than 1,000 people and most of the people knew one another by name or at least by reputation. One day a bully approached me in school to give up my lunch; I told him my name and warned him I had five older brothers, who would take care of him, if he did not leave

---

[105] Hebrews 13:5
[106] Italics supplied
[107] Romans 8:38-39

me alone. Once he realized I was related to those five guys, he quickly backed-off and nothing, more was said to me about giving up my lunch to him or anyone else. With Jesus comes this same kind of assurance. It is wonderful to know that God provides that same sense of protection and security to His bride, the church.

In one instance He says,

> You yourselves have seen what I did to Egypt, and how I carried you on eagles' wings and brought you to Myself. Now if you obey Me fully and keep My covenant, then out of all nations you will be My treasured possession...[108]

The Psalmist actually paints a vivid picture of God's protection toward those He loves.

> The Lord is my light and my salvation -- whom shall I fear? The Lord is the

---

[108] Exodus 19:4-5

stronghold of my life -- of whom shall I be afraid? When evil men advance against me to devour my flesh, when my enemies and my foes attack me, they will stumble and fall. Though an army besieges me, my heart will not fear; *though war break out* [109]against me, even then will I be confident. [110]

There is nothing more thrilling, especially to a woman, than to know she is loved and protected by the man in her life. A man being loved and knowing he has the means wherewith to protect his loved ones has to be equally gratifying.

God has both the desire and the ability to be to you, whatever you need Him to be, at whatever time you need Him to be there. He will gently soothe your sorrows with reminders of former answers to prayer as a basis to believe. He will presently answer your prayers again.

---

[109] Italics supplied
[110] Psalms 27:1-3

When you come confessing your faults, which you know have pained Him terribly, He will lovingly "rock you in the cradle of His love", as the song says, eagerly and attentively listening to whatever you have to say; patiently waiting for you to finish a thought without interrupting. Then affectionately He will turn your attention again, to His written word, where He says,

> If we confess our sins, he is faithful and just and will forgive us our sins and purify us from all unrighteousness. [111] My son, do not make light of the Lord's discipline, and do not lose heart when He rebukes you, because the Lord disciplines those He loves, and He punishes everyone He accepts as a son. [112]

---

[111] I John 1:9 NIV
[112] Hebrews 12:6 NIV

Then afterwards, he exhorts you with such tenderness, that you cry like a baby in its mother's arms.

A novel thought relative to having intercourse with God is that there is never a need to worry about infections or STDs. The thing you need to concern yourself with is **not** getting infected with HGP - *Holy Ghost Power*! You **want** to be infected with HGP, so you can pass it on to others. When you intercourse with God, there is no fear of physical mishaps to frustrate you, if you are a woman, or to upset you, if you are a male. God never has mishaps; He is consistent and He will stay by you, until you are satisfied and at peace.

When you intercourse with God, women you do not need to fear pregnancy and men do not need to fear that they might be trapped. Rather, both should long to become pregnant with His promises that they might bear the fruits of righteousness.

When you intercourse with God, there is no place for embarrassment: for there is no comparison to former or present lovers;

no pressure to experience anything earth shattering and no excuses about anyone's inability to perform to your standards. It is just the two of you enjoying intimacy at the highest, yet the most basic level.

The famed psychologist, Abraham Harold Maslow, founder of the Humanistic Psychology Movement, developed a human needs chart, which depicts five levels of humanity's needs. The first or basic level includes food, clothing, shelter and sex. Succeeding levels include safety and love; and the highest level is humankind's need for self-actualization.[113] When you copulate with God in earnest prayer, you experience all five levels at the same time. Hallelujah! What kind of man is this? He is the Son of Man, who has **All Power!**[114]

#

---

[113] The World Book Encyclopedia, World Book, Inc. Vol. 13 p. 265 - Scott Fetzer Co., Chicago - London -Sydney - Australia
[114] Matthew 28: 19

BARRIERS TO EMPOWERMENT

What is empowerment and how does it relate to being intimate with God? Good question! Empowerment is the noun formed from the transitive verb empower, which means to give power to; to give official authority or legal power to <someone>; to enable; to promote the self-actualization or influence of <someone or some organization>.

Empowerment can only be extended by someone or some organization that has greater authority, power or dominion than the person or thing to which the empowerment is given.

When one is empowered, he/she is given a grave responsibility. Empowerment is not designed to be hoarded, to be kept to one's self and to be used selfishly for one's own personal benefit, but rather it is given that one might take charge of and care for other things or persons who have need of the gifts you have to offer. **In other words, to**

grant one empowerment is to call one into service; it is to extend to them privilege.

When one enters the chamber of our Lord Jesus, one is given the precious privilege to first acquaint one's self with the knowledge of the heart of God, His precious love for humanity and His desire to salvage all who are willing to come. Moreover, with that knowledge, one is called into the service of God to become an instrument for use. We talked about this briefly in the chapter, *Approaching The Throne*. However, for the purpose of this chapter, we shall focus our attention on a parable Jesus gave to us in Matthew 25:14-18 of a lord and his three servants.

> For *the kingdom of heaven is* as a man traveling into a far country, *who* called his own servants, and delivered unto them his goods. And unto one he gave five talents, to another two, and to another one; to every man according to his several ability; and straightway took his journey. Then he

that had received the five talents went and traded with the same, and made *them* other five talents. And likewise he that *had received* two, he also gained other two. But he that had received one went and digged in the earth, and hid his lord's money.

Jesus gave us this parable to teach us many lessons, such as: occupy until He returns in the clouds of heaven; use what God has given you, as well as, to teach us habits of industry and faith. However, there is another lesson that can be drawn from this parable and that is how well does the servant know His master? How intimately had they become acquainted before the master left on His journey?

It seems obvious that each servant had some prior knowledge of his lord, because they were employed in his service. No one works for another for any length of time without becoming vaguely aware of the type of employer for whom he/she works.

Therefore, based on the *perception* each person had of his lord, each one of them went to work to use or not to use the talent[s] given him. But one's *perception* is ***not true reality***. It merely constitutes that particular person's reality.

What am I trying to say here? I'm saying that each servant had his own perception of his lord, which constituted his reality; and each person worked within the perception of reality that he had. However, the wrong perception can be a barrier to empowerment and as such, a threat to one's salvation. Now let us look more closely at the parable and see what it reveals about the barriers and one's intimacy with God.

The person with five talents perceived that his lord was a fair and generous man: one who was willing to finance or back the efforts and ideas of a conscience, hardworking, ambitious person. Consequently, he went out and doubled his talents. How had he arrived at this conclusion? Obviously, he had taken the time to intimately acquaint himself with his lord. He had observed how his lord related to others in business or personal relationships. Perhaps he had sought counsel from his lord about the best way to approach his tasks, while in his lord's service. It seems that he may have shared with his lord some ideas that could advance his lord's business, for had he not received the most talents? Perhaps, he had voiced to his lord during a conversation or maybe many conversations, his desire to follow in his lord steps someday.

However, despite what may or may not have taken place between the two of them, his lord had developed a relationship with him that had garnered confidence. He believed that by empowering this particular servant with the most talents, he would in turn reap the most benefits. Therefore, without hesitation or apology, he promoted and empowered this servant with the greatest talents.

Considering that this is a spiritual lesson being taught here about Jesus and his followers, it could be said of this servant, as it was said of Abraham:

> For I know him, that he will command his children and his household after him, and they shall keep the way of the LORD, to do justice and judgment; that the LORD may bring upon Abraham [that servant] that which he hath spoken of him. [115]

This servant had scored high on his lord's list and his lord was not going to allow his servant to go un-noticed or un-empowered. He had proven himself, worthy of trust, for he had taken the time to get to "know" his lord.

Although the servant who received the two talents had doubtless experienced several of the opportunities the first servant had. However, it appears that he was not held at the same level of esteem as the first, for he had received fewer talents. Yet, he

---

[115] Genesis 18:19

proved faithful to his task, doubling the talents as did the first. He perceived that his lord was a fair and patient man: one who would not overload his servants with too many tasks, so that success would be out of his reach, but would rather grant an opportunity to broaden one's perspective, and to make a name for one's self in the process. Therefore, he too, went and doubled his talents, using his more limited abilities.

The servant with only one talent perceived that his lord was a hard, uncaring man: one who was insensitive to the needs of others, but only looked to receive whatever he might be able to get for himself. He thought the landlord to be mean, greedy and overbearing: a man who expected to reap, even though he had not sown. Look at how he addresses the man upon his return.

> Then he which had received the one talent came and said, **Lord, I knew thee that thou art an hard man, reaping where thou hast not sown,**

and gathering where thou hast not strawed: And I was afraid, and went and hid thy talent in the earth: lo, *there* thou hast *that is* thine.[116]

He had decided not to let his lord take unfair advantage of him. He would not do all of that extra work trying to develop the talent given. After all, since his lord was not going to be there watching him, then he could take a few more breaks and not have to work as hard as usual. He could sit back and let others do the bulk of the work. He would just do those specifically assigned tasks he was hired to do, and take care of those things that did not involve having to do any extra work such as trying to develop a talent. So, he hid it for safe keeping, until his lord would return. Surely, there could be no wrong in that! But there was some wrong; much wrong!

I believe the one talent given to this servant was the talent of time. Now I don't have any Scripture to back me up on this

---

[116] Matthew 25:24-25

one, but God has given to every man a measure of faith [117] and a talent. In order for everyone to have a fair chance at developing that talent, it had to be equal to everyone else's. Hence, we all have 24 hours in a day, and seven days in a week. But you may ask how can one make more time? One cannot necessarily make more time, but one can maximize the time one has.

For example: I could go over to the church alone, and spend three hours dusting, vacuuming, mopping and cleaning the washrooms and kitchen. Or, I could enlist the service of one other person and between the two of us we could get the job done in one and one-half hours. Moreover, if there were three of us, it could be done in one hour. That would allow me to have one to two hours to do something else of value. The more people that are involved, the less time each one needs to spend individually working on any one task. By developing time management skills one can accomplish

---

[117] Romans 12:3

more in three hours than others accomplish in eight. That is developing the talent.

Later, when the lord returned and everyone else was being empowered with prestigious positions and rewards, this servant was being demeaned, and demoted. Why? Let's break down those barriers to this servant's empowerment and then make the spiritual application to ourselves.

1. He did not appreciate his association with his lord. He failed to spend time to get to know him, so that he could learn to trust his lord's heart.

God has called us to be co-laborers together with Him. But how can we co-labor properly, if we fail to intercourse/converse with Him who has all of the plans?

God has called us by his own name: Christian. But many of us take His name in vain by not living up to His standards – commandments. If we ignore or neglect the time we could be interfacing with Him by spending that time on countless other matters, we defame His name. Often after a long and hectic day, we neglect time with

God when that is the time we need to spend with Him the most. Only He can bring the help and comfort that we crave during those situations.

Christ has redeemed us with His own blood. However, do we really take the time to contemplate what that means in reality?

> Christ manifested his interest in the salvation of every soul. When he endured the death of the cross, he made provision for the pardon of every soul, and to those who would obey his commandments, he promised eternal happiness in his kingdom. How is it that so few respond to this love? God is our creator, and we are dependent upon him for every blessing, for shelter and food and clothing, for religious opportunities, for the grace we enjoy; and yet how cold are our hearts! Many are even led to behold Calvary, they are pointed to the crucified Saviour, and yet they are unmoved by the manifestation of

Infinite Love. But shall we look with stoical indifference upon all the revealing of his love? Rather, shall not our hearts be melted and subdued in fervent gratitude and love? Shall we not sing the praise of our Creator and Redeemer? God has endowed men with emotional powers, and these are to be exercised and strengthened, but many seem to be devoid of feeling. They manifest no gratitude; give no praise to God, the giver of all their mercies. They display affection toward their friends, but the great Source of all blessing, the gracious Benefactor, receives not that love to which he is entitled. All heaven looks with amazement upon this unnatural exhibition of ingratitude toward Him who sends his sunshine and rain on the evil and on the good. [118]

---

[118] E.G. White, Signs of the Times, January 5, 1891 - Pacific Press, Mountain View, CA

2. The servant did believe in his lord. Neither do many of us. Jesus declared that we can become partakers of the divine nature [119] – but we reject it. We fail to believe the wonderful promises God has declared in His Word; we doubt Him constantly. How can intimacy be established in the face of disbelief and doubt? It cannot be; there is no vulnerability, which is the basis of true intimacy.

Jesus declares that He is coming again soon; watch for the signs – but too often, by our actions, we scoff as much as the world does at His coming, as seen by our own activities. Compare the time you have studied His Word, in the last 24 hours, against the time you have engaged in non-essential activities. Remember, we all have the same 24 hours and 7 days.

Jesus declares that we are to love each other as members of our family – but we can barely speak to each other civilly, sometimes, much less love one another.

---
[119] II Peter 1:4

Carefully read this next quote; it's a sad commentary for Christians.

> Paul admonishes the early church communities to avoid the deterioration of personal relationships in the "body of Christ." Many interpersonal difficulties come from tearing each other down and in the process, hurting the entire community. People who engage in gossip and backbiting tend to have problems themselves – feelings of inferiority, the need to be noticed, a desire for control or power, and other insecurities. These people need help to abandon this hurtful way of dealing with their inner conflicts. [120]

All of these are definite barriers to empowerment or service to God.

3. The servant's perception of his lord was all wrong. He perceived his lord to be

---

[120] Adult Teacher's Sabbath School Lesson, 1st Qtr. 2011, General Conference of SDA, pg.50

like himself: lazy, uncaring and selfish. The enemy of souls does everything he can to keep our attention diverted in any other direction than toward God. As long as we fail to seek God wholeheartedly, we shall possess a narrow, negative image of Him. When in reality, we are really casting our eyes upon the adversary; again, a definite barrier to empowerment!

The servant mistook an opportunity to grow, as one of inconvenience. If you will remember, I spoke of being hesitant at times to get out of bed in the middle of the night and pray, however, God showed me those were the times when He could best reveal Himself to me. On the surface, it may appear to be inconvenient to spend time developing intimacy with God, but that is just a trick of the enemy. As long as he can keep you deceived about how wonderful God really is, the more entrapped you will be by him.

4. The servant boasted that, "he knew" his lord, but he did not really know him at all.

> Not everyone that saith unto me, Lord, Lord, shall enter into the kingdom of heaven; but he that doeth the will of my Father, which is in heaven. Many will say to me in that day, Lord, Lord, have we not prophesied in thy name? and in thy name have cast out devils? and in thy name done many wonderful works? And then will I profess unto them, **I never knew you**: depart from me, ye that work iniquity. [121]

In the Day of Judgment, Jesus will declare of many, "I never knew you". I never married you; I never inter-coursed with you; we were never intimate! Depart from me, ye workers of iniquity (lawlessness): those who failed to keep His commandments.

    5. This servant was fearful, but of what? Was he fearful of success because it would mean more responsibility? Was he fearful of failure, because he thought it would cause him embarrassment? Moreover,

---
[121] Matthew 7:21-23

was he fearful of being taken advantage of? You know, John, the Revelator tells us that the fearful and unbelieving will be on the outside of the city with the lost ones. [122]

6. This servant was rebellious, which made him wicked. He knew his lord expected him to do something with his talent, but he rebelled against doing it. The Prophet Samuel declared that rebellion was as the sin of witchcraft [123] – now that is wicked!

7. Lastly, this servant was lazy and unwilling to do his part. His lord called him a "wicked and slothful servant." To be slothful is to be "extremely or habitually indolent." You never, if you can get out of it, do anything to help in God's service.

He was lazy; he hated work. He just wanted to stand around and talk. Did you notice how many more words he used than those who had been productive? When all is said and done, there was more "said" than "done".

---

[122] Revelation 21:8
[123] I Samuel 15:23

God seeks to empower each of us with His Holy Spirit that we might learn to draw nearer to Him. The closer we come to Him, the more spiritual authority He will extend to us. We will be like the first servant, to whom He gave the five talents. Why? Because like the first servant, we will have taken the time to know Him intimately; He will give us the greater number of the talents and through the power of the Holy Spirit, we too, will yield Him perfect service. Then upon His return, He will say to us:

> ...Well done, *thou* good and faithful servant: thou hast been faithful over a few things, I will make thee ruler over many things: enter thou into the joy of thy lord

#

BREAKING THE CHAINS

This is a very grave chapter. It deals with subject matter that I would much rather bypass. In fact, I wrestled with the Lord about this chapter, because I know that some will be offended by its boldness. Some will say that I am sitting in judgment; others will say that it is not my business and they will be right. It is not MY business; it is GOD'S business. However, in this book, I am commissioned to speak for God and I refuse to be like the servant with one talent. I refuse to lose my empowerment for failing to be faithful to my calling. Although, I am not a prophet, I feel compelled, by the Spirit of God to share the information in this chapter. Therefore, I stand on the following warning given in the book of Ezekiel:

> Again, the word of the LORD came unto me, saying, Son of man, speak to the children of thy people, and say unto them, 'When I bring the sword upon a land, if the people of the land

take a man of their coasts, and set him for their watchman: If when he seeth the sword come upon the land, he blow the trumpet, and warn the people; Then whosoever heareth the sound of the trumpet, and taketh not warning; if the sword come, and take him away, his blood shall be upon his own head. He heard the sound of the trumpet, and took not warning; his blood shall be upon him. But he that taketh warning shall deliver his soul. **But if the watchman see the sword come, and blow not the trumpet, and the people be not warned; if the sword come, and take any person from among them, he is taken away in his iniquity; but his blood will I require at the watchman's hand.' So thou, O son of man, I have set thee a watchman unto the house of Israel; therefore thou shalt hear the word at my mouth, and warn them from me. When I say unto the wicked, O wicked man, thou shalt**

surely die; if thou dost not speak to warn the wicked from his way, that wicked man shall die in his iniquity; but his blood will I require at thine hand. Nevertheless, if thou warn the wicked of his way to turn from it; if he do not turn from his way, he shall die in his iniquity; but thou hast delivered thy soul.[124] (boldness added)

It is in the light of this Scripture that I pen this chapter. By God's grace, I shall blow the trumpet and warn those who read this chapter and are guilty, of their sins; for I do not want anyone to be lost, nor do, I want the guilt of anyone's blood upon my hands. Therefore, I shall proceed to define the chains; instruct how-to break them; how-to keep them broken and to point out the relevance all of it has to intimacy with God.

I have learned that God has created some of the most out of the ordinary creatures; there is one reference, in the book

---
[124] Ezekiel 33:1-9

of Ezekiel, which describes a magnificent creature with four faces:

> And I looked, and, behold, a whirlwind came out of the north, a great cloud, and a fire infolding itself, and a brightness *was* about it, and out of the midst thereof as the colour of amber, out of the midst of the fire. Also out of the midst thereof *came* the likeness of four living creatures. And this *was* their appearance; they had the likeness of a man. And every one had four faces, and every one had four wings. And their feet *were* straight feet; and the sole of their feet *was* like the sole of a calf's foot: and they sparkled like the colour of burnished brass. And *they had* the hands of a man under their wings on their four sides; and they four had their faces and their wings. Their wings *were* joined one to another; they turned not when they went; they went every one straight

forward. As for the likeness of their faces, they four had the face of a man, and the face of a lion, on the right side: and they four had the face of an ox on the left side; they four also had the face of an eagle. Thus *were* their faces: and their wings *were* stretched upward; two *wings* of every one *were* joined one to another, and two covered their bodies. And they went every one straight forward: whither the spirit was to go, they went; *and* they turned not when they went. [125]

Isn't that fascinating? Here Ezekiel sees four creatures; all of them were the same type of creature. Each one had four faces (man, lion, eagle and ox), one on each side of the creature. All of them had wings, which were joined to each other. Under their wings were hands like that of a man and although their wings stretched upward, two additional wings covered their individual body. From the sound of it, their feet, which

---

[125] Ezekiel 1:4-12

looked like that of a calf, were described as if they stood up on their toes. When they traveled, they never turned around; they simply traveled in the direction of that particular face. Amazing!

Another attention-grabbing creature that God made was Lucifer, one of the covering cherubs that stood beside the very throne of God and sang Holy, Holy, Holy. Look at some of the captivating features about this creature.

> ...Thou sealest up the sum, full of wisdom, and perfect in beauty. Thou hast been in Eden the garden of God; **every precious stone *was* thy covering, the sardius, topaz, and the diamond, the beryl, the onyx, and the jasper, the sapphire, the emerald, and the carbuncle, and gold**: the workmanship of thy tabrets and of thy pipes was prepared in thee in the day that thou wast created. Thou *art* the anointed cherub that covereth; and I have set thee *so*:

thou wast upon the holy mountain of God; thou hast walked up and down in the midst of the stones of fire. Thou *wast* perfect in thy ways from the day that thou wast created, till iniquity was found in thee. [126] (boldness added)

Again, there are some things about this creature that are definitely unique. He is said to be perfect in his ways; that his tabrets (some have said this represented his ability to sing all the different chords of music at the same time) were built into him at his creation. However, the part that I find the most intriguing is that of his covering, or his skin, (as we would call it, for that is what we have) was made out of various kinds of beautiful reflective jewels and gold! Can you imagine that? The equivalent of his skin was jewels! Surely, he was beautiful, in the beginning.

All of these creatures described in Scripture, thus far, are truly stunning.

---

[126] Ezekiel 28:12-15

However, when God decided to make man, He did something uniquely different; watch:

> And God said, **Let us make man in our image, after our likeness**: So God created man in his *own* image, in the image of God created he him; male and female created he them.[127]

Here we see God electing to do something totally different! Instead of making man to appear like some other very unusual creature (at least to us, anyway) God elected to make us look like Him. What a marvelous compliment! Of all the creatures in the universe that we know about we are the only ones said to reflect the image of the Creator Himself. But wait; there is more to this story.

> And the LORD God formed man *of* the dust of the ground, and breathed

---

[127] Genesis 1:26-27

into his nostrils the breath of life; and man became a living soul. [128]

I have no idea how God created those other creatures. He may or may not have spoken them into being, much like He did the animals and water creatures that exist on this earth; that is not for us to know. However, the record states that when He created man, there was quite a bit of personal interaction going on in the process. Scripture states that "we were formed", which implies to me some "hands on" activity. Next, He specifically and very intentionally breathed into man's nostrils the breath of life, which indicates a deep level of intimacy to me. I can imagine God holding Adam closely in His arms and leaning over to place His mouth over his nostrils; then very carefully and deliberately, breathing rhythmically into those newly formed nostrils until He could feel the breath coming back into His own face. Yes, man was especially made. But that's not all:

---

[128] Genesis 2:7

And the LORD God said, *it is* **not good that the man should be alone; I will make him an help meet for him**...And Adam gave names to all cattle, and to the fowl of the air, and to every beast of the field; but for Adam there was not found an help meet for him. And the LORD God caused a deep sleep to fall upon Adam, and he slept: and he took one of his ribs, and closed up the flesh instead thereof; And the rib, which the LORD God had taken from man, made he a woman, and brought her unto the man. And Adam said, This *is* now bone of my bones, and flesh of my flesh: she shall be called Woman, because she was taken out of Man. [129]

God wanted man to reflect Himself; therefore, He took great pains to ensure that it was so. After Adam had finished naming all of the created animals, he realized that

---

[129] Genesis 2:18, 20,21-23

there was not among them, anything with whom he could be intimate. Nothing was reflective of him. There must have been a longing in his heart for a mate; all of the animals had one. How do I know? I know, because the record reflects that Adam named them all and how would we know to call a female deer a doe, instead of a buck, if Adam had not given her the name?

Anyway, God created a very special someone for Adam; so special until he called her after himself, indicating the closeness that should be shared between them. Even though she was taken out of man, she was distinctively different from man. However, her anatomy was specifically fashioned to compliment his. Additionally, from the intimacy they would share, the earth would be populated.

Things in the garden were perfect, until a malefactor entered and set things upside down!

Now the serpent was more subtle than any beast of the field, which the

LORD God had made. And he said unto the woman, Yea, hath God said, Ye shall not eat of every tree of the garden? And the woman said unto the serpent, We may eat of the fruit of the trees of the garden: But of the fruit of the tree which *is* in the midst of the garden, God hath said, Ye shall not eat of it, neither shall ye touch it, lest ye die. And the serpent said unto the woman, Ye shall not surely die: For God doth know that in the day ye eat thereof, then your eyes shall be opened, and ye shall be as gods, knowing good and evil.

And when the woman saw that the tree *was* good for food, and that it *was* pleasant to the eyes, and a tree to be desired to make *one* wise, she took of the fruit thereof, and did eat, and gave also unto her husband with her; and he did eat. And the eyes of them both were opened, and they knew that they *were* naked; and they sewed fig leaves together, and made themselves aprons.[130]

Did you notice that Adam and Eve did not even realize that they were naked until they ate the fruit! Surely, they had been around each other long enough to notice the absence of clothing? Unless they were covered with something else; look at this: **"Who coverest *thyself* with light as *with* a garment:"** [131]

The Psalmist is describing God's clothing – garments of light. If God covers Himself with light and Adam and Eve were made in His image after His likeness, it stands to reason that they, too, were covered with light, and thereby did not see each other's nakedness. However, when they fell from grace, the light of righteousness departed and they stood naked before each other; hence, their response to God.

---

[130] Genesis 3:1-7
[131] Psalms 104:2

And they heard the voice of the LORD God walking in the garden in the cool of the day: and Adam and his wife hid themselves from the presence of the LORD God amongst the trees of the garden. And the LORD God called unto Adam, and said unto him, Where *art* thou? And he said, I heard thy voice in the garden, and I was afraid, because I *was* naked; and I hid myself. And he said, Who told thee that thou *wast* naked? Hast thou eaten of the tree, whereof I commanded thee that thou shouldest not eat? And the man said, The woman whom thou gavest *to be* with me, she gave me of the tree, and I did eat. And the LORD God said unto the woman, What *is* this *that* thou hast done? And the woman said, The serpent beguiled me, and I did eat. [132]

The wily foe, (Lucifer, turned Satan and using the serpent as a medium), had

---

[132] Genesis 3:8-13

beguiled Eve into eating from the forbidden tree, and she, in turn, seduced Adam; now, the couple hides, transgressors of God's law. They have switched masters, but God would not give up on them so readily. First, He promised to send them a savior, next He administered their punishment, beginning with Adam, who must now till the soil to make a living; next, to Eve, who would have difficulty delivering babies and lastly to the snake that had consented to be used as a medium; hereafter, he would crawl upon his belly. Also, God told Satan that he would ultimately come to ruin. Then, as any loving father would do, God did something special: **"Unto Adam also and to his wife did the LORD God make coats of skins, and clothed them."** [133]

God was left with no other choice, other than to destroy them, but to put them out of the garden; He said:

> ...Behold, the man is become as one of us, to know good and evil: and

---
[133] Genesis 3:21

> now, lest he put forth his hand, and take also of the tree of life, and eat, and live forever: Therefore the LORD God sent him forth from the garden of Eden, to till the ground from whence he was taken. [134]

God is heartbroken; the one creature that He has made "like unto himself, in His image", has misused his free will and has fallen from his exalted position. The enemy felt that he had won a great victory over God, and from that point on he has put forth his every effort to efface (to wipe out, to obliterate, to remove without a trace, to rub out, to smooth away, to destroy) the image of God in man. Therefore, he has devised many, many chains in which to enslave humanity in his effort to accomplish this one goal. Despite the many sub-chains that exist, technically, there are only three main chains. They can be summarized by the Apostle John's description in the following text:

---

[134] Genesis 3:22-23

Love not the world, neither the things *that are* in the world. If any man love the world, the love of the Father is not in him. For all that *is* in the world, **the lust of the flesh, and the lust of the eyes, and the pride of life,** is not of the Father, but is of the world. [135]

These chains are summed up as: the lust of the flesh; the lust of the eyes and the pride of life. These three things cover all of the sins that are committed in the world; it does not matter which sin you might name, it falls in one of these three categories. Now, that we have covered that, let us look at some of the items which fall under these three categories and are presently plaguing God's people. Everyone has been bound with some type of chain, at one time or the other. However, there is freedom to be had despite the type of chain. Therefore, let us investigate a few.

---

[135] I John 2:15-16

Under the category of the flesh, we will probably find the greatest number of chains.

Appetite is probably the supreme chain. It was upon appetite that our forefathers fell and it was upon appetite that Jesus gained His first victory in the wilderness, after His baptism. Take a look:

> Then was Jesus led up of the Spirit into the wilderness to be tempted of the devil. And when he had fasted forty days and forty nights, he was afterward an hungered. And when the tempter came to him, he said, If thou be the Son of God, command that these stones be made bread. But he answered and said, 'It is written, Man shall not live by bread alone, but by every word that proceedeth out of the mouth of God'. [136]

It was important that Jesus meet and defeat the foe on the same ground whereby

---

[136] Matthew 4:1-4

our fore parents had fallen. However, they were not hungry, just curious. Jesus, after 40 days of fasting was near starvation when the tempter arrived. Angels had visited Christ from time to time and when the enemy showed up, he doubtless was as beautiful as those who still minister about God's throne. However, he gave himself away in his very first sentence to Christ. He said, "If thou be the Son of God..." Satan had been successful in getting Eve to question and then doubt God's word at the tree; he had said to her, "...hath God said, ye shall not eat of every tree of the garden?" Causing her to question; now he tried to get Christ to question whether or not He was really the "sent of God". However, God had confirmed at Christ's baptism that "He was His beloved Son" and the Holy Spirit had descended as a dove and lighted upon His shoulder in added confirmation. Therefore, Jesus had no reason to doubt that He was who He claimed to be.

However, the enemy finds a far more ready participant in us, when it comes to partaking of things that are contrary to us. Among the prime health destroyers are **sugar, fat and salt**. Food manufacturers have so saturated the market with food items laden with these three ingredients, which causes obesity, diabetes and hypertension, not to mention the MSG (mono sodium glutamate), which makes food addictive to the taste buds and the majority of us have fallen victim to the enemy's plan to efface the image of God in us to some degree.

In addition to that, when God gave instructions to the Israelites to eat only clean meats and avoid others, as outlined in chapters 14 of Deuteronomy and 11 in Leviticus, God specifically told them also that they were to **eat no blood or fat** from the animal or they would be cut off from God's people; that means loss of salvation.[137]

They were to cut the throat, allow the blood to drain, wash the animal and then prepare it for food. But how many people do you know that actually do this, even among

---
[137] Leviticus 7:23-27

Christians? God said, the "life is in the blood." [138] Yet there are people who will refuse blood transfusions, using that selfsame reason, and conversely, eat rare beef. The blood was sacred, for it was what atoned for sin.[139] These are chains, people.

The second biggy in this category is forbidden sex. There are any number of directions I could go from here, but allow me to touch on three of them.

a) Homosexuality and lesbianism has exploded exponentially in this country in the last 10 years or so. I do not need to give anyone stats on this; it is everywhere we turn: on television, in our schools, in legislative offices and a plethora of other places. Many of our children and adults are confused about their sexual identity. These are not bad people, just confused and misinformed people.

Well, please let me help out those of you who might be reading this chapter. If you will recall at the first part of this chapter

---

[138] Leviticus 17:11
[139] Leviticus 17:11 & Hebrews 9:22

when I spoke of God creating woman for man, God created the female to be a **complimentary asset** to him. She has openings that he does not have, which allow access to appendages that he has, but are missing on her. By bringing these openings and appendages together, at the right time of the month, the creative process, which God installed in the two of them can unite in populating the earth, as God designed it to be. No two same sex individuals, despite their ingenuity, can duplicate the Master's plan. Am I making myself clear? The enemy has created this forbidden sex union so as to destroy God's physical, mental, spiritual and emotional image in humanity. Not to mention, look at how God sees it:

> Thou shalt not lie with mankind, as with womankind: it *is* abomination.[140] (outrage, disgrace, scandal, atrocity)
>
> Don't have sex with a man as one does with a woman. That is

---

[140] Leviticus 18:22 – KJV Bible

abhorrent[141] (repugnant, objectionable, repulsive, disgusting)

For the invisible things of him from the creation of the world are clearly seen, being understood by the things that are made, *even* his eternal power and Godhead; so that they are without excuse: Because that, when they knew God, they glorified *him* not as God, neither were thankful; but became vain in their imaginations, and their foolish heart was darkened. Professing themselves to be wise, they became fools, And changed the glory of the uncorruptible God into an image made like to corruptible man, and to birds, and four-footed beasts, and creeping things. **Wherefore God also gave them up to uncleanness through the lusts of their own hearts, to dishonour their own bodies between themselves:** Who changed the truth of God into a lie,

---

[141] Leviticus 18:22 – The Message Bible

and worshipped and served the creature more than the Creator, who is blessed forever. Amen. **For this cause God gave them up unto vile affections: for even their women did change the natural use into that which is against nature: And likewise also the men, leaving the natural use of the woman, burned in their lust one toward another; men with men working that which is unseemly, and receiving in themselves that recompense of their error which was meet. And even as they did not like to retain God in *their* knowledge, God gave them over to a reprobate mind, to do those things which are not convenient;** Being filled with all unrighteousness, fornication, wickedness, covetousness, maliciousness; full of envy, murder, debate, deceit, malignity; whisperers, backbiters, haters of God, despiteful, proud, boasters, inventors of evil things, disobedient to parents, without understanding, covenant breakers, without natural affection, implacable, unmerciful: Who knowing the judgment of God, that they which commit such things are worthy of death, not only do the same, but have pleasure in them that do them.[142]

Bottom line: God loves humanity, which is sinful and undone, but He hates the "sin", for it is reflective of the nature of Satan and not of Himself. God is a Holy, righteous God, which cannot bear to look upon sin. This being the case, how does one who engages in this type of activity expect to develop an intimate relationship with Him? He cannot, until his heart is truly willing to forsake this activity. And if you think it cannot happen, keep reading.

b) Bestiality is another form of forbidden sex. We look at certain entertainment figures, such as Miley Cyrus,

---

[142] Romans 1:20-32

and we see this type of sin being pushed into the faces of young children and adults who follow her image. Truthfully, this is equally as gross as homosexuality and lesbianism, if not more so. And don't fool yourself, God has something to say about this also:

> Neither shalt thou lie with any beast to defile thyself therewith: neither shall any woman stand before a beast to lie down thereto: it *is* confusion. Defile not ye yourselves in any of these things: for in all these the nations are defiled which I cast out before you: And the land is defiled: therefore I do visit the iniquity thereof upon it, and the land itself vomiteth out her inhabitants [143]
>
> Don't have sex with an animal and violate yourself by it.
>
> A woman must not have sex with an animal. That is perverse.

---

[143] Leviticus 18:23-25 – KJV Bible

"Don't pollute yourself in any of these ways. This is how the nations became polluted, the ones that I am going to drive out of the land before you. Even the land itself became polluted and I punished it for its iniquities—the land vomited up its inhabitants. [144]

Notice how God not only strictly forbids this activity; He explains to the Israelites that this is why the Lord drove out the nations that occupied the land before they arrived. This says to me that if America continues to engage in this type of sin, it too, will be abominable in the sight of God and we are seriously running the risk of losing all of the privileges presently bestowed upon us. God is not going to continue to be mocked! Especially those who claim to be His people need to seriously make things right between them and God that they might be delivered from the soon coming destruction upon this land. Seek, even now,

---
[144] Leviticus 18:22-25 The Message Bible

to develop an intimate relationship with Him.

c) Fornication/adultery is a sin that has been so grossly indulged, even by Christians that it is lightly considered by most of us today. Even having children out of wedlock is not looked upon as something to cause shame among us. The baby is gladly welcomed among the congregation and ooed and ahhed over and made to feel as though he were from a legitimate royal family. And, although I agree; did you read that? I agree the baby should be loved and coddled and made to feel special, however, the parent(s), who are members of the congregation, need to be disciplined.

As Christians, we say we believe in the 10 Commandments, or God's moral law. Are we to pick and choose which commandment we are to obey? Are they not all equal? Did He not write all 10 of them in stone, indicating that they could not be changed? Then if we would discipline a member for worshipping a wooden image, worshipping Baphomet, killing someone, or embezzling money from their job or the church, should we not discipline someone, whom we know, is committing fornication or adultery? Are we to just pick and choose which commandments to obey, or are we to obey them all? If Jesus said we are not to do it, then we are not to do it! Paul says we should "flee fornication", [145] and surely we are to respect the marriage bed and not commit adultery. You decide how you think it should be done. I believe you have my answer. I am not trying to be unkind or heartless; we have all sinned and come short of the glory of God. However, when the sin is obvious, for the sake of those who could be led astray by the failure of the church to take action, I say, let us stand up for Jesus, in a kind and loving manner and apply the needed discipline. Here is my last comment on this. I will let Paul settle the matter:

> Ye have not yet resisted unto blood, striving against sin. And ye have forgotten the exhortation which

---

[145] I Corinthians 6:18

speaketh unto you as unto children, My son, despise not thou the chastening of the Lord, nor faint when thou art rebuked of him: For whom the Lord loveth he chasteneth, and scourgeth every son whom he receiveth. If ye endure chastening, God dealeth with you as with sons; for what son is he whom the father chasteneth not? But if ye be without chastisement, whereof all are partakers, then are ye bastards, and not sons. Furthermore, we have had fathers of our flesh, which corrected *us*, and we gave *them* reverence: shall we not much rather be in subjection unto the Father of spirits, and live? For they verily for a few days chastened *us* after their own pleasure; but he for *our* profit, that *we* might be partakers of his holiness. Now no chastening for the present seemeth to be joyous, but grievous: nevertheless afterward, it yieldeth the peaceable fruit of righteousness unto them, which are exercised thereby. Wherefore lift up the hands which hang down, and the feeble knees; And make straight paths for your feet, lest that which is lame be turned out of the way; but let it rather be healed. Follow peace with all *men*, and holiness, without which no man shall see the Lord: [146]

The lust of the eyes encompasses far more than I could address in this one chapter. It could literally fill a book. However, I would like to mention the entertainment industry, especially movies and television. Admittedly, there are some decent things on television. God has blessed many Christian networks to arise and share much regarding the matter of salvation and souls have been won for the kingdom of God. However, we must be careful to guard the avenues of the soul (eyes, ears, mouth, smell and taste) so that we are not encumbered by the things of the world and

---

[146] Hebrews 12:4-14

thus fail of meeting Christ's demand for our loyalty.

In some online research, I learned that television has a hypnotizing effect on the mind. Once we begin to watch it, no matter what it is we are watching, we fall into a hypnotic state after just three minutes of viewing. This leaves us open and vulnerable to be programmed to believe and to act upon whatever information is being transmitted to us by the program we are watching. If it is good information, then it might not be so bad. But how much of what we watch is really that good?

I know I have been guilty of watching programs, in the past, wherein the main characters were made to look like heroes, but they had to kill people or rob a bank, etc., and I would find myself rooting for them. Or a man and woman would face so many difficulties trying to get together and become a couple, until when they would finally get together, even consummating their affections outside of marriage, there was a sense of happiness for them in my heart. And of course, there are all of those detective shows where they look for the bad guys, but someone always has to get murdered first. One pastor termed it "Worshipping at Satan's throne". However, the Apostle John shares some sobering information regarding this conduct, not on the program's part, but on mine:

> Blessed *are* they that do his commandments that they may have right to the tree of life, and may enter in through the gates into the city. For without *are* dogs, and sorcerers, and whoremongers, and murderers, and idolaters, and **whosoever loveth and maketh a lie**. [147]

Did you get that last part? "Whosoever loveth and maketh a lie". Whether you are the liar or the one that loves the lie (ungodly fiction), you will find yourself in the lake of fire. That Scripture woke me up to the reality that I was as verily

---
[147] Revelation 22:14-15

committing the sin, by enjoying it as it was unraveled before me, as were those who were engaged in it. The Holy Spirit spoke to me one day and said, "How long are you going to watch these things, until Jesus comes?" As I thought about the question, I had to think seriously about my actions. Then He brought that Scripture to my mind and I shuddered! Did I really want to be lost for watching Desperate Housewives, or Friends or any other of these contrived and outlandish programs? I did some serious confessing and repenting. I went into my Father's throne room and found the help, strength and comfort I needed to walk away. So can you.

One more thing: this following statement really sobered me up concerning this matter:

> When the thought of evil is loved and cherished, however secretly, said Jesus, it shows that sin still reigns in the heart. **The soul is still in the gall of bitterness and in the bond of**

iniquity. He who finds pleasure in dwelling upon scenes of impurity, who indulges the evil thought, the lustful look, may behold in the open sin, with its burden of shame and heart-breaking grief, the true nature of the evil, which he has hidden in the chambers of the soul. 'The season of temptation, under which, it may be, one falls into grievous sin, does not create the evil that is revealed, but only develops or makes manifest that which was hidden and latent in the heart. As a man 'thinketh in his heart, so is he,' for out of the heart 'are the issues of life.' [148]

Lastly on the list of chains is the pride of life. You know it was pride that caused Lucifer's downfall. Let us look at it:

---

[148] E.G. White – Thoughts From the Mount of Blessing, pp. 59,60 - Pacific Press, Mountain View, CA

How art thou fallen from heaven, O Lucifer, son of the morning! *How* art thou cut down to the ground, which didst weaken the nations! **For thou hast said in thine heart, I will ascend into heaven, I will exalt my throne above the stars of God: I will sit also upon the mount of the congregation, in the sides of the north: I will ascend above the heights of the clouds; I will be like the most High.** Yet thou shalt be brought down to hell, to the sides of the pit. [149]

He had some very high ambitions and some serious "I" problems. The greatest one being that he thought he could exalt his throne above the stars of God, sit in the highest place of worship among all the created beings, which God had made and be as powerful as God. My, my, my! Foolish creature.

---

[149] Isaiah 14:12-15

However, although most of us do not have such high ambitions, we can become exceedingly proud about our new house, car, position of employment, even position in the church. We sometimes become boastful of our business or social connections, our places of travel, our educational achievements and a thousand other things; you name it, it exists. We too easily fall into the enemy's trap of pride, thus perpetuating the chains that bind us to him.

Nevertheless, before I leave this last category regarding chains, to go on to, how they can be broken, I must mention jewelry, piercings and tattoos. The wearing of jewelry has reached an all-time high in the world today. There was a time when mostly women were the ones who wore it and that rather modestly, with perhaps a ring and small matching earrings or perhaps a broach on occasions. Now everyone, just about, at all levels and all ages; men, women and children are covered with all kinds of jewels, real and fake. The enemy has convinced so many that the "bling bling" is the way to go.

He wants them to look as he does, completely enshrouded with reflective jewels and gold, instead of looking modestly as Jesus did when He walked the earth; another blow at effacing the image of God in man.

When we examine the "woman" of Revelation 12, which represents the pure church, she is modestly appareled with the sun, moon and stars. When we examine the "harlot" or false church of Revelation 17, it says, "The woman was arrayed in purple and scarlet colour, and **decked with gold and precious stones and pearls**..." This should clearly give us an indication as to where we should stand, if we profess Christ as Lord of our lives.

Many do not realize it, but piercing the ears is a sign of a slave submitting to his/her master. Let us read about that.

> When you buy a Hebrew slave, he will serve six years. The seventh year he goes free, for nothing. If he came in single he leaves single. If he came

in married he leaves with his wife. If the master gives him a wife and she gave him sons and daughters, the wife and children stay with the master and he leaves by himself. **But suppose the slave should say, 'I love my master and my wife and children— I don't want my freedom,' then his master is to bring him before God and to a door or doorpost and <u>pierce his ear with an awl, a sign that he is a slave for life</u>.** [150]

By piercing yourself, you are making yourself a slave to the one who inspired your piercings. You are choosing whom you will serve.

When it comes to tattoos, one can hardly see the true skin color on many of our athletes, because there are so many tattoos on them. I am sure many athletes and perhaps even you have never read this text of Scripture:

---

[150] Exodus 21:2-6 – MESSAGE Bible

Ye shall not make any cuttings in your flesh for the dead, **nor print any marks upon you:** I am the LORD. [151]

Much like the commercial for Prego sauce, "it's in there". Whatever you need to know about how to earnestly serve and please God can be found in the Word of God. We might have to search for it, but He will lead us into all truth; that's one of the reasons we need to develop an intimate relationship with Him, so that He can reveal many of the things that otherwise would lie hidden from us.

We need to be very careful: Proverbs 5:22 states, "His own iniquities shall take the wicked himself, and he shall be holden with the cords of his sins."

It is our iniquities, those things that we know we should not do, but we keep repeating and make plans to repeat; these are the chains that will bind us to the enemy, efface the image of God in us and cause the

---

[151] Leviticus 19:23

loss of our ultimate salvation. Nevertheless, it does not have to be like that.

Victory over every chain that has bound us can be broken, through our faith and cooperation with the Holy Spirit. Watch the miracle:

> Now when they heard *this*, they were pricked in their heart, and said unto Peter and to the rest of the apostles, Men *and* brethren, what shall we do? Then Peter said unto them, Repent, and be baptized every one of you in the name of Jesus Christ for the remission of sins, and ye shall receive the gift of the Holy Ghost. For the promise is unto you, and to your children, and to all that are afar off, *even* as many as the Lord our God shall call. [152]

Praise God! When the people heard the gospel preached unto them and had their sins pointed out to them, it says that they

---

[152] Acts 2:37-39

were pricked in their hearts: conviction came to them. If you have read this chapter and found yourself guilty of any of the things mentioned, such as myself, then allow the Lord to convict your heart and be willing to turn from your iniquities. Following is a revelation followed by a marvelous promise and a reality check:

> If we say that we have no sin, we deceive ourselves, and the truth is not in us. **If we confess our sins, he is faithful and just to forgive us our sins, and to cleanse us from all unrighteousness**. If we say that we have not sinned, we make him a liar, and his word is not in us. [153]

Acknowledgement, sorrow for sin and confession; these are the steps to be taken to receive forgiveness and cleansing. Here are yet some more wonderful promises that should help us make that break:

---

[153] I John 1:8-10

> He that covereth his sins shall not prosper: but whoso confesseth and forsaketh *them* shall have mercy. Happy *is* the man that feareth alway: but he that hardeneth his heart shall fall into mischief. [154]

Again, we are given both sides of the issue that we might make an intelligent and righteous decision for God regarding getting any chain broken. Now let us briefly discuss how to keep the chains broken. Let us cling to this promise for deliverance.

> By entering through faith into what God has always wanted to do for us—set us right with him, make us fit for him—**we have it all together with God because of our Master Jesus.** And that's not all: We throw open our doors to God and discover at the same moment that he has already thrown open his door to us. We find ourselves standing where we always

---
[154] Proverbs 28:13-14

hoped we might stand—out in the wide open spaces of God's grace and glory, standing tall and shouting our praise. There's more to come: We continue to shout our praise even when we're hemmed in with troubles, because we know how troubles can develop passionate patience in us, and how that patience in turn forges the tempered steel of virtue, keeping us alert for whatever God will do next. In alert expectancy such as this, we're never left feeling shortchanged. Quite the contrary—we can't round up enough containers to hold everything God generously pours into our lives through the Holy Spirit![155]

Hallelujah! Can't you feel those chains dropping? Can't you hear them crashing to the floor? Doesn't that Scripture give you a sense of freedom and victory? "We have it all together with God", it

---

[155] Romans 5:1-5 – The Message Bible in Contemporary Language

declares, because of our Master Jesus. Is Jesus your master? If not, He can become it today, even now, if you will seek an intimate association with Him. Then if you do, you may rely on the following promises to keep you free of any chain forever.

> But if we walk in the light, God himself being the light, we also experience a shared life with one another, as the sacrificed blood of Jesus, God's Son, purges all our sin. [156]

> But God be thanked, that ye were the servants of sin, but ye have obeyed from the heart that form of doctrine which was delivered you. Being then made free from sin, ye became the servants of righteousness. [157]

> But thank God you've started listening to a new master, one whose

---

[156] I John 1:7
[157] Romans 6:17-18 - KJV Bible

commands set you free to live openly in his freedom! 158

Now unto him that is able to keep you from falling, and to present you faultless before the presence of his glory with exceeding joy, to the only wise God our Saviour, be glory and majesty, dominion and power, both now and forever. Amen. 159

And now to him who can keep you on your feet, standing tall in his bright presence, fresh and celebrating— to our one God, our only Savior, through Jesus Christ, our Master, be glory, majesty, strength, and rule before all time, and now, and to the end of all time. Yes. 160

---

[158] Romans 6:17-18 - The Message Bible in Contemporary Language
[159] Jude 24-25 - KJV Bible
[160] Jude 24-25 – The Message Bible in Contemporary Language

Let us claim complete victory together in Jesus Christ, who is able to break every chain from His children and keep them broken, as long as we maintain an intimate relationship with Him. Hallelujah!

###

DRAW NEAR TO GOD

The psalmist wrote in Psalm 73:28, "It is good for me to draw near to God", and hopefully you are learning how good it is for you to draw near to Him also. A relationship with God begins when God calls us or draws us. [161] Jesus said, "No one can come to Me, unless the Father, who sent Me, Draws him; and I will raise him up (resurrect him) at the last day." [162]

After God calls us, He expects us from then on to exercise the idea in seeking to draw near to Him. If we do, we have this very encouraging promise: "Draw near to God and He will draw near to you." [163]

The promise of a resurrection to life after death becomes a primary motivator. The Apostle Paul calls it that "better hope, through which we draw near to God."[164]

---

[161] Jeremiah 31:31
[162] John 6:44
[163] James 4:8
[164] Hebrews 7:19

As we seek to develop this overall intimate, personal relationship with God, it might be easier for some of you to look at an orderly list of suggestions for achieving this most important goal.

Pray: Prayer is simply carrying on a conversation with God, the same way you communicate with anyone else you love. Prayer helps you to explore your relationship with God. Just like any relationship, learning to know and be known by God takes time – a lifetime. Make time each day to visit with God. Share your thoughts and listen for God's words for you.

Study: Start with reading and then expand it into running reference texts. It's amazing what you will discover when you begin to dig into the Word of God for yourself and not to just listen to the preacher or the Bible teacher.

Worship: Worship and praise draw you into the very throne room of God. The Psalmist tells us that "God inhabits [lives in] the praises of Israel [His chosen people]." [165]

---

[165] Psalms 22:3

Praising God, thanking God, giving God your attention is an important part of feeling closer to the One who created, redeemed and sustains us. How and where you choose to worship is personal, sometimes in community [church] and other times in private. Worshipping and honoring God connects us to God's ongoing work in the world and refreshes our souls.

Fellowship: Spending time with friends, family and our faith community adds richness and depth to our lives, just as God intended. We were created for community. Paul's first letter to the Thessalonian church shares these thoughts:

> We always give thanks to God for all of you and mention you in our prayers constantly, remembering before our God and Father your work of faith and labor of love and steadfastness of hope in our Lord Jesus Christ. [166]

---

[166] I Thessalonians 1:2-3

We are all in this together, sharing space and sharing our lives. God's gift of fellowship helps us to realize the importance of each of us and how we each contribute to God's purpose as a whole. When we gather in fellowship we remember that God is with us, indeed, with all of us.

Serve: While fellowship reminds us we are a part of a larger purpose, service is the gift we give to that purpose. What are your favorite things to do? What are you passionate about? Chances are, with prayerful thought, you can find some great ways to share God's loving spirit with those around you in ways that tap into your gifts to serve. When we each serve with our individual gifts, God is always there to celebrate with us.

Listen: Sometimes it is important to stop talking, stop mentally analyzing and just listen. Close your eyes, hear what is going on around you and be wherever you are. Listening can awaken all of our senses as to who God is in our lives. Hearing the wind whistle around your house during a storm, a siren in the distance or a dog barking in your neighbor's yard speaks of God in nature, God's presence in times of need and God's love in a kind companion. Where else can you hear God? Learn to close your eyes and listen.

Reflect: Meditation and reflection on your relationship with God will dazzle and delight you! Why? Giving yourself permission to appreciate that God created you, God loves you, God redeems and sustains you every moment of every day of your life is exhilarating. You belong here, nestled in the strength and beauty of God's love because you are a part of God's creation. How does that make you feel? Think about it.

Repent: How is it possible for a mortal human to have an intimate and ongoing relationship with the divine God? The most important key is God's gift of His Spirit to swell in one's heart and mind! God's Spirit works to transform human nature to a godly nature and the mind of Christ; so instead of being inclined to selfishness and sin, we become inclined toward love and godliness.

> Then Peter said to them, 'repent and let every one of you be baptized in the name of Jesus Christ for the remission of sins; and you shall receive the gift of the Holy Spirit. [167]

We cannot receive a greater gift than the Holy Spirit. Jesus said He would be our teacher, our guide, our convincer in error and our comforter in times of distress. He has been sent to aid us in our preparation for heaven. Why not ask God to imbue you, even now, with His presence, so that you might be better fitted today to follow Christ than you were yesterday. Jesus will always answer, "Yes" to that request. Ask Him now.

#

---

[167] Acts 2:38

SPIRITUAL "QUICKIES"

Have you ever seen an elderly woman sitting with her eyes closed, tears streaming down her cheeks, her hands tightly clasped together, as she rocks back and forth? Sometimes her lips are moving, sometimes they are not, and from her innermost spirit, come forth sounds of moaning or simply "Ump, ump, ump". Do not bother her; she is in his chamber inter-coursing/communing with God. Perhaps she could not find a closet right then, but she needed to spend time with her man, Christ Jesus. It does not matter when or where you are, if you need a "quickie" or you plan to stay awhile, he promises never to turn you away.[168]

Do you remember the biblical character Hannah? She was the wife of Elkanah. She was distressed because she had no children. Her husband's second wife, Peninnah, had given him several children,

---

[168] St. John 6:37

and she would often tease Hannah about being barren.

Well, one year when Hannah and her husband went to the temple in Shiloh to appear before the Lord, Hannah was too distraught to eat. Instead, she decided she would go and talk with God about this matter of being barren. She needed help and she needed it, right then!

Therefore, she went to a quiet area in the temple and prayed sincerely to God for a child, promising that she would give the child back to God for his entire life. As she prayed, her lips moved but no sound came out. She was in His chamber.

The High Priest witnessed her earnestness in prayer and mistook it for drunkenness. He went to her, burst in upon her, in her openness with God; interrupted her intercourse with the one true love that she had, and reproved her for being drunk. Pulling her spiritual garments about her, to cover her vulnerability, she explained her situation and convinced him she was not drunk, but merely troubled. However, God used that priest to send His answer to Hannah immediately. "Go in peace: and the God of Israel grant thee thy petition that thou hast asked of him." "...So the woman went her way, and did eat, and her countenance was no more sad."[169] She left her lover, Jesus, satisfied and happy.

Now when you consider this issue of "quickies" strictly from a human point of view regarding relationships, it may or may not convey the idea of satisfaction, especially for the female. Many times in the course of your busy schedule, you may find yourself sexually frustrated, with no foreseeable opportunity to spend a quality weekend, or even an evening for that matter, with your mate. The only chance you might have time to be with him/her is in the "quickie" mode. I remember one of my married, adult, daughters told me that she had a sign, which hung in her kitchen that read, **"Sex is a misdemeanor: the more I miss the meaner I get."** If that is your

---

[169] I Samuel 1:1-18

case, then a quickie might be your best answer.

Have you ever seen Christians with their faces twisted up like prunes? They seem to be living examples of my daughter's sign about misdemeanor. For them, **prayer is a misdemeanor:** the more they miss, the meaner they get. They have not realized that prayer to God brings sunshine into the soul and spreads joy all around.

However, let us look at what a "quickie" implies. Since prayer is an intercourse with God, then it means not only are you going to communicate with him, and that intimately, you will be looking for a favorable or satisfactory response. If you have the time and the opportunity, it is to your benefit to take advantage of it, and pour out your soul to the master and wait for a response. Nevertheless, sometimes time is not on your side and you need help right now! Let us look at a few more examples of *spiritual quickies*.

Again, in the Old Testament, we find Joshua and the children of Israel fighting against five kings[170] who had conspired together, to overtake the city of Gibeon. The inhabitants of Gibeon had tricked the Israelites into making a pact with them. They promised to be the Israelites servants, if the Israelites would spare their lives; and the Israelites had done so. Now Gibeon was in trouble and needed the Israelites to deliver them.

Joshua and the Israelites honored the pact, despite the trickery. Moreover, when the Israelites went to Gibeon to save them from the five-king invasion, God promised to deliver those kings into Joshua's hand. However, in the process of fighting against them, the sun began to set and Joshua felt that their armies would get away if something drastic did not happen. Therefore, he sent up a "quickie" prayer unto God. He cried, "Sun stand thou still upon Gibeon; and thou Moon, in the valley of Ajalon." That is all he said, and the Scriptures record that the sun stood still and did not go down for nearly an entire day.

---

[170] Joshua 10:1-15

Read it for yourself! It was a "quickie", but it brought the required results.

There is another situation presented in the book of Nehemiah. [171] Nehemiah was King Artaxerxes' cupbearer, and was ever to be joyful in the presence of the king; much like everyone else was required to be. However, after hearing some bad news about his homeland, Jerusalem, he was troubled and his mind filled constantly with how to rectify the existing situation? Many Jews had returned to Jerusalem, after their 70 years of captivity by Babylon, yet they had not rebuilt the temple or the walls of the city. One day when Nehemiah appeared before the king, his face reflected his inner feelings. When the king noticed it, Nehemiah became afraid, and he said, "So I prayed to the God of heaven."

Here this man was, standing in the presence of the king trying to compose himself so that he could give the king an intelligible answer to what was causing him grief. He did not have time to formulate any

---
[171] Nehemiah 2:1-8

long, beautifully articulated words, to find some immediate clarification to his situation. He sent up a "quickie" prayer and God gave him satisfaction.

One of my favorite examples of a "quickie" is the Apostle Peter drowning in the Sea of Galilee.[172] The disciples had been obedient to Christ. Following his command to cross the sea to the other side, they got into the boat and began their journey. During the course of their crossing, however, the wind became extremely active causing the sea to become boisterous. The disciples were wrestling with the boat, trying to keep it from capsizing, when they spotted what appeared to be a ghost coming toward them. As they cried out in fear, Jesus said, "Be of good cheer; it is I; be not afraid."

One would think that after Jesus identified himself to the disciples that they would leave it at that, calm down and everything would be fine once again. Jesus had done so many miracles in their sight,

---
[172] St. Matthew 14:22-33

and he had just earlier that day fed five thousand men, plus women and children, with just a handful of food; surely walking on the water should not have caused them to be so astir. However, Peter, ever pushing the proverbial envelope, challenged Jesus to give him the power to walk on water, if he was in fact who he said he was. Jesus granted his request. However, when a wave came between him and his master, his faith failed and he began to drown. He offered up the shortest "quickie" in Scripture. "Lord, save me!" Was he saved? You bet he was! He was saved and satisfied.

# # #

ARE YOU STILL A PRAYER VIRGIN?

When a female has sex for the first time, quite often, but not always, the hymen, which is the thin mucous membrane that closes part or sometimes the entire opening of the vagina is broken, which causes her to bleed slightly from the intrusion. It represents a female's transition from the girl status, to that of a woman. It forever changes her. A maiden in Scripture was very careful to preserve this occasion for her husband. She would even place a cloth beneath her on her wedding night, to catch the blood, and she would give this cloth to her parents for safekeeping. This was the "token of her virginity." [173] It was extremely important.

As a child growing up, we referred to this experience as "bursting your cherry". If a female was a virgin, then it was presumed that her "cherry" was still intact, and she was thought of as a "good girl", or "naïve"

---

[173] Deuteronomy 22:13-17

and "inexperienced". During that era, it was something about which one was to be proud, because the "first" time was special and was to be reserved for one's husband.

In this spiritual parallel, there are many of you who have yet, to burst your cherry. Some of you, despite the fact that you have engaged in prayer on some occasion, are still considered *spiritual prayer virgins*. You have yet to experience the intrusion of God into your heart, your life, your very being. You are holding yourself in reserve, afraid to allow such intimate acquaintance, with the God of heaven, for fear it will change you. You want to keep your life orderly and tidy: everything in its own place. Thus *you* can maintain control of things, you think!

However, those of you who have ever had sexual relations know there is no such thing as "tidy" sex, especially if you want to receive fulfillment. In the course of the interchange, somebody's hair is going to get ruffled; there will be much perspiration expended and a great deal of energy spent;

much like the night spent in the Garden of Gethsemane.

In the Garden of Gethsemane, Jesus told all but three of his disciples, to wait for him near the entrance, to the garden. He took those three, Peter, James and John, and went farther into the Garden; but then, he left them at a different spot, and went "… about a stone's cast…" [174] away, so he could be alone with his lover (God).

While there, the story says that he wrestled with his lover, engaging in deep sensual intercourse, to the point that "… his sweat was as it were great drops of blood falling down to the ground." [175] He went into his "closet", the very chamber of God, and earnestly, passionately beseeched the father that he might not have to die such an excruciating shameful death. He cried, "Saying father, if thou be willing, remove this cup from me: …"[176] He was defenseless, he was exhausted, he was open and

---

[174] Luke 22:41
[175] Luke 22:44
[176] Luke 22:42

vulnerable to the father's wishes. The powers of hell were pressing in upon him, seeking to discourage and dissuade him from the challenge, of being man's sacrifice for sin. Despite his own desires, despite his own need to be satisfied, he was willing to satisfy the father, whether he received reparation or not; for he went on to say, "… nevertheless not my will, but thine be done." [177] He totally yielded to the wishes of the father; it was his desire that the father be pleased and happy, in this exchange. As a result, "… there appeared an angel unto him from heaven, strengthening him." [178] It was only after he had completely and without reserve, yielded to his father that he climaxed, and in turn received the fulfillment he craved.

In order to reach total realization in any communication or intercourse both parties will have to put forth a lot of selfless effort to please the other. There is no place for, "I'll get mine now, and you can get

---

[177] ibid
[178] Luke 22:43

yours later"; which so many try to do with God. They hurriedly blurt out their requests, not giving themselves time to hear from God; to see what's on His mind or agenda for them for that day or situation; that is the worst kind of intercourse and leads to gross miscommunication and frustration; especially on the part of God. However, if you extend yourself, spend some time meditating and listening for His voice as revealed in His Word, or the inmost part of your being, surely, at the end of the communiqué, both parties will have changed a bit, and will be happy about it.

The prophet Isaiah speaking of this intercourse in the Garden of Gethsemane said:

> Yet it pleased the Lord to bruise him; he hath put him to grief: when thou shalt make his soul an offering for sin, he shall see his seed, he shall prolong his days, and *the pleasure of the LORD shall prosper in his hand. He*

> *shall see of the travail of his soul, and shall be satisfied:* ... [179]

Satisfied!

Yes, if done correctly, everyone will be satisfied. There will be feelings of endearment, happiness and joy that will follow a sweet sense of contentment, and a desire to recommit oneself to the other, as in the case with Jesus and his father.

In a loving committed relationship, no one is seeking to control the other person. Each person is submitting himself/herself to his/her respective mate, to achieve perfect harmony. Each person has the same goal: to give pleasure as well as to receive it. Ultimate communication is attained, if both parties are willing to give themselves up to uninhibited passion, as Jesus did.

The same theory holds true for you, when inter-coursing with God. You must not be overly concerned with what it is you want or need. You must not be demanding or dictating in the exchange. You must not

---
[179] Isaiah 53:10-11 (Italics supplied)

inhibit your passion, but come before him boldly. Willingly offer up your heart, your desires, and your plans. Ask him to have his way with you and keep nothing in reserve, and you will experience both spiritual and physical release.

Did you notice that the physical release Jesus sought, did not come until he had gone in unto the father three separate times, asking for the same thing, over and over and over again. He was determined not to walk away discontent. Much like Jacob, when wrestling with the Angel (God) by the brook Jabbok, Jesus' soul cried out, "...I will not let thee go, except thou bless me." [180]

Sometimes you may have that same cry. At times, you may be approached in the middle of the night, as was Jacob. Situations may appear gloomy or portentous. All of your careful planning and preparation may collapse at your feet. You realize that your only hope is in Jesus. Therefore, you slip out of your bed and enter your prayer closet. Sometimes you might have to weep and

---
[180] Genesis 32:25

moan; sometimes perspiration may drop from your pores, as you wrestle with him for answers; you may have to spend all night in prayer. You may even realize the need for fasting, in order to receive the satisfaction you desire: but it is worth it. Joy will come in the morning. He will turn your enemies into friends or make them your stepping-stool.

Be assured, there is nothing noble, virtuous or righteous about being a "virgin" with God. He wants you to be experienced. He wants you to be unreserved. He wants to share with you all-embracing passion; this is the only way you will find ultimate happiness. Please, burst your spiritual cherry with God. Move from maidenhood into womanhood, move from boyhood, to manhood. You will never be the same, you will change forever, and you will be overjoyed that you did.

###

P.U.Y.S.S.

There is a very popular acronym, which you doubtless have heard: it is PUSH. It means Pray Until Something Happens. I think that is a wonderful philosophy. However, the Lord has given me a different one to share with you: it is PUYSS. It means Pray Until Your Soul's Satisfied. I mean pray until you have reached a spiritual crescendo with Jesus.

One morning, prior to the day scheduled for this message at the prayer breakfast, I woke up about 3:30 a.m. At first I resisted getting up, but the Lord carefully reminded me that I could not effectively talk to anyone about being approached in the middle of the night by Him, or approached before the sun was up, and of having a satisfactory experience, unless I was engaging in the act myself. Therefore, I asked Him to forgive me and to wake me up completely that we might interface better. So He woke me up and communed with me intensely for the next several hours, to the point that by 6:30 a.m. (a time I never get up to eat) I was cooking breakfast - famished from my time spent with him, but satisfied for the moment.

Then I thought about why people have prayer breakfasts. Some say morning is the best time of the day to engage in intimate exchange. While others prefer mid-week night prayer, so they can sleep a little bit better. However, the truth be told, anytime with Jesus is the best time. He will put a smile on your face and a skip in your step. He will have you singing, for no apparent reason to others, but you will know what has taken place between the two of you, and your song will be, "Tis Sweet, I Know."

Anyway, after breakfast, I tried to lay down a little while longer, (my day normally starts around 9 a.m.), but as soon as I lay down, He called me forth again: filling me with fresh ideas and integral insights into His love. Therefore, I take no credit for this book. He got me up in the middle of the night, and has kept me up on different occasions filling my mind with thoughts that needed sharing.

I have found that God is assertive, but not aggressive. He will come back repeatedly seeking my company, wanting to know if it is all right if we spend some time together. If I refuse, by turning my attention to something else, and not interfacing with Him, He will step back and let me go my way. Yet, in His mercy, He will return again and again gently urging me to come into His chamber for a repast. When I finally consent, He lays out a scrumptious meal, in His Word, and whispers sweet promises in my ear.

I've learned that God invites me continuously into His presence, because he doesn't want me to be tempted by other lovers; to be drawn away by less satisfying more demanding suitors who mean me no good. He wants me to know that He is the best thing that has ever happened to me. He goes out of His way to prove His love to me on a continuous basis that my heart might be "fixed" [181] on Him.

However, let me caution you about something. Many people believe that when they pray, their lives will suddenly get easier and their problems will all go away. If that is what you are thinking, or if that is what you think, I am advocating, then you are dead wrong.

Often when you pray, your life will seem to get far worse than it has ever been. You have the best of intentions, when you start praying. You pray and ask God for a closer walk with Him. You ask Him to reflect more of Himself through you than He has in the past. You tell Him that you want to be wholly His, and that you have lain all upon the altar. "Use me, Lord", you plead. Then you sit and wait for your life to become a proverbial "bed of roses". Well do I ever have news for you!

Think for a minute about what you are really saying to God. You are telling Him to shine through you, and that you have laid

---

[181] Psalms 108:1

everything on His altar. However, what kind of altar is that exactly? It is an altar of sacrifice! [182] It is an altar for the burning of dead carcasses. The sacrifice to be offered, has had its throat cut, all of its blood drained from its body, it has been cut into pieces and now it is on the altar to be burned as a sweet smelling savor unto God. Moreover, you wonder why your life suddenly turns upside down, after you pray that prayer. In order for God to answer your prayer requests, you are going to have to experience "death to self" first. There is no other way to put it.

Remember, Jesus is the "Lamb of God" who has taken away the sins of the world. In order for Him to have done that, he had to be sinless, which called for a life of severe restraint, self-denial, patience, long-suffering, and the ability to take abuse. After that, He died. Therefore, if we continue with this line of thinking, then you too will have to die. You will have to die to your own wishes, over others. You will have to die to your self- indulgence; die to

---
[182] Romans 12:1

your own "pity parties"; die to the pain of insults; die to slights by others; and die to unkind words and all manner of evil humanity is capable of heaping upon you (and there is an awful lot of heaping that can be done). You will have to learn to keep quiet,[183] when you want to let it all hang out and rip someone to shreds with words or even with your hands, because of what they may have said or done. It is not easy!

You have prayed, "Lord let your life be reflected more fully in me". In order for light to reflect through an object, one of two things must take place with the object: either the object must be porous enough -- meaning to have enough holes in it - so that the light can shine through; or it must be sheer enough -- meaning pure -- for the light to shine through it. Either way, the ability for the light to shine through an object is dependent on the object. Therefore, since you are the object, and you want Jesus to reflect more fully in you, the object must be prepared, so the light can shine through.

---
[183] I Thessalonians 4:11

The light does not need any preparation, it will shine anywhere, whether seen or not. The *object* is the problem.

Hence, when you pray for Christ to fully reflect in you, you are really asking God to prepare you to house His light. You are saying, "God put some holes in me, make me more transparent. Tear down my walls of defense; knock out my blocks of bullishness; scrape away my sarcasm; chisel out my cheating; stretch me to my limits so that I can be thinner and sheerer; pound me; bruise me; recreate this object, which is like cement - set in its way - unmoving, ungiving." Is it coming clear to you yet? It is not easy.

You give God permission to go to work on a major reconstruction project, which is going to take time to frame and fashion. There is going to be a lot of hammering some sense into your head; a great deal of sawing away your bad habits; and some major sandblasting of your old ideas about who He is and how He works. In order for Him to undertake this project, He must choose the right tools for your transformation. Sometimes His tools come in the form of loss -- death of loved ones, loss of money or spouse. Other times it may come in the form of a prejudiced supervisor, a cantankerous co-worker or a spiteful "saint". Nevertheless, it comes, if you are patient, willing and prayerful, if you turn to God for your security and strength, then the reform will move along nicely, and you will be given strength to bear it all. However, if you fuss, cuss, and complain, it makes progress exceedingly slow and extremely painful.

God only wants the very best for you, and I am convinced He will do anything, short of breaking His own commandments, in order to revamp and save you. Therefore, if you will consent to the makeover, He will polish you after the similitude of a palace. [184] He will wax and buff, scrub and shine, wash and rinse you, until you are perfectly

---

[184] Psalms 144:12

clean, and can be placed in His coffer where all the other precious jewels are kept. [185]

So, be careful how you pray, and for what you pray. Do not just say something you have heard others say before, because it sounds good and it will make you appear noble, if it comes to pass. Be practical and patient when you pray to God. He ever sits and waits to hear your earnest prayers, they are like sweet incense unto Him and He does not take them lightly. He does not take pleasure in your pain, but much like a paramedic has to hurt you, in order to put a splint on your broken leg, so God has to allow hurt to you in order to place a spiritual splint on your broken life.

Therefore, pray much, ask God to show you for what to pray and how to pray; that is what the disciples did. [186] Are you not a disciple? If you are, why wait? Fall on your knees and plead with the Father to open your eyes and let you see yourself as He sees you. Then ask Him for the strength to

---
[185] Malachi 3:17
[186] Luke 11:1

remove from your life, anything that is not like Him, or with which He is displeased. Take one thing at a time, so that you will not be overwhelmed. Be consistent with your prayer, and gradually you will begin to see changes, but not without conflict, hurt, or some remorse. Nevertheless, as you pray, God will give strength to sustain you as He gave to Jesus in Gethsemane. [187] Remember, He does not willingly afflict or grieve you. [188] He is merely answering your prayers. Therefore, pray! Yes, **P.U.Y.S.S. -- pray until your soul's satisfied.**

#

---

[187] Luke 22:42-43
[188] Lamentations 3:33

PUBLIC AFFECTION

Praying in public is equivalent to being out with your mate, in a public place. People who see you together can tell you have an intimate relationship by the way the two of you interact. When a couple is in love with each other, they enjoy being together. It does not matter so much in what activity they are engaged, just so long as they are engaged in it together.

You may catch the two of them walking along holding hands, with a sense of security in their relationship. Perhaps you might see them standing close beside each other talking in low discreet tones. The male may inadvertently slip his arm around his mate's waist, while observing some activity performed by others, or her hand might naturally come to rest upon his shoulder, as she looks on. The physical exchanges between them are natural, yet judicious. They know who they are, and are comfortable with their relationship.

Although they are keenly sensitive to the other's needs and desires, there is no need on the part of either one of them, to engage in overt or improper physical affection. To do so would be sensational and exhibitionistic.

They are in love, tenderness and affection for one another is always sensitive and respectful of the presence of others. They know the joy and satisfaction they seek to bring to each other, in the privacy of their boudoir. However, they also know what is proper and improper to say and do in the company of onlookers: they keep private matter private, as it should be.

That is what public prayer is to be like. Whenever you pray publicly, always be discreet. Keep your personal prayers on a generic basis and focus on the reason for the public prayer. Lift up to God those reason and any persons associated with the reasons.

Keep private things private when you address God in public. Those who see and hear you will be keenly aware that you have an intimate relationship with Jesus. As Luke describes it in Acts, [189] they should know "...you've been with Jesus and learned of his ways." The smile of contentment He has left on your face should be evident for all to see.

There are times, when in public, you might just whisper, "Thank you Jesus", or "Lord have mercy", or perhaps "Hallelujah". These are all expressions of your affection toward him and the intimacy you share. However, never become vulgar in your prayers, by stating all of your business, or the private affairs of others, for whom you pray in secret. It is, totally, unacceptable, and is much like watching a couple "French kiss" on a subway, in a restaurant or a grocery store, while they grope one another. It is reprehensible for them to do it, and embarrassing for those who watch.

Seek to avoid spiritual voyeurism, also. When you find people praying inappropriately in public, turn your thoughts to the reason you are there praying. Try not

---

[189] Acts 4:13

to listen to all of the revealed secrets of others, by these vulgar, exhibitionistic prayers. If necessary, begin to pray for the person that is praying. Ask God to reveal to him/her the things that need addressing and to stop incongruously exposing confidential matters.

God is a respectful, discreet God. He does not reveal your secrets to others. He does not flaunt His interactions with you, in the face of other individuals. Remember, He has encouraged you to go into a closet, when you pray, which indicates the level of privacy he desires you to have with him. Therefore, we all need to honor that, as far as possible.

###

THE GREAT FEAR

"You will hear of wars and rumors of wars, but see to it that you are not alarmed..." [190] "...men's hearts failing them for fear of those things..."[191]

Jesus has warned humanity of some tragic events, which will come upon the world, and rightly so. We can all be grateful for the warnings He has given relative to the end of all things that we might be prepared when they happen. However, there is also a great fear in the communication area, of which we need to take note.

According to Dr. Phil McGraw, author, psychologist and famous television guru, *rejection* is man's worst fear, when it comes to women. He stated, in a very recent television broadcast, that men are sometimes afraid to approach women they really would like to be with, for fear that they might not

---

[190] Matthew 24:6 NIV
[191]

be able to "bring to the table", those qualities they feel that particular woman requires or demands. Consequently, this fear of rejection, on the part of men, helps to perpetuate the miscommunication process, which exists between the genders already.

Rejection is a hurtful, humiliating emotion, which no one wishes to experience. Rejection says, "You're not good enough"; "you're not acceptable"; "you're not desirable"; "you're worthless"; "you're substandard"; "you're not believable"; "you're not trustworthy"; and a thousand other things, programmed into your thinking, based on your own rejection experiences. Yet, rejection is something God endures every day.

Humankind's refusal to submit to God's continuous call to repentance, fellowship, and a love relationship with Him, says to God, "you're not good enough"; "you're not acceptable"; "you're not desirable"; "you're worthless"; "you're substandard"; "you're not believable"; "you're not trustworthy". Although there is no fear in God, as He continues to pursue humankind, there is a great deal of pain and regret in His heart.

The first regret we witness on God's part, says, "And it repented the LORD that He had made man on the earth, and it grieved Him at his heart." [192]

Humanity was still fresh from the Master's hands, when the firstborn of Adam and Eve, became a murderer. The entire course of humankind became repeatedly worse, until God decided to put an end to the loose, lewd way humanity was behaving; and the grievous, ungrateful manner they chose to misuse the abundance of gifts God had given them. The Word declares:

> And God saw that the wickedness of man was great in the earth, and that every imagination of the thoughts of his heart was only evil continually. [193]

Thus, God declared humankind must

---
[192] Genesis 6:6
[193] Genesis 6:5

be destroyed, with the exception of Noah and his family, and so He chose a flood, as his destructive device.

Men may become intimidated and fearful of approaching women, in an effort to develop a relationship, for fear of rejection; but God is bold and pursues humankind with a stark determination. "Come unto me, all ye that labor and are heavy laden, and I will give you rest. Take my yoke upon you, and learn of me; for I am meek and lowly in heart: and ye shall find rest unto your souls. For my yoke is easy, and my burden is light."[194] God knows what He can "bring to the table". He knows what it takes to relieve, refresh and revamp His pursuit. He knows that a relationship is based on two people voluntarily committing to share in an intimate loving relationship, where both are pulling together, in the same direction, effectively communicating, to get a job done. He graciously invites us to enter into a twosome, and to get to know him better. He says that when we do this, we

---

[194] Matthew 11:28-30

will find that it is better than we ever expected, it will be, far more enjoyable than we ever anticipated, and it is far less stressful than going it alone.

He uses the metaphor of two yoke-pulling oxen, together, side-by-side, step-by-step, in harmony, one with the other, to illustrate how easy a relationship can be -- how to have a satisfying spiritual intercourse: good communication, with Him.

Good communication--intercourse-- the act of communicating between two or more persons: the interchange of ideas, feelings or services is aptly illustrated by the yoke metaphor. When two people begin any project together, there will be a period of adjustment. No two people are so suited together, as to never have any conflict or are so duly matched that they can skip the adjustment period. Even with the best of circumstances, each person needs to get to know the other: to identify their strengths and weaknesses, that each might be able to balance the other, in some way. However, it does not stop with the adjustment period, for people grow and change; so does a good relationship. Jesus said, "...learn of me..." [195] To learn means to study; to spend some time endeavoring to know better; to investigate what causes one to tick or what motivates, excites or disappoints the other.

In the act of getting to know one another, one must engage in communication, for it is the very core of relationships. Once any two people have resolved the communication issue, the relationship will flourish, and the two become stronger than either one could alone. Therefore, God invites us to come to Him in prayer, the first step in the communication process: that all-important first step in relationship development. He encourages us,

> Come now, and let us reason together, saith the LORD: though your sins be as scarlet, they shall be as white as snow; though they be red like crimson, they shall be as wool.[196]

---
[195] ibid
[196] Isaiah 1:18

God knows who you are, faults, failings and all, and he still pursues you, saying, "Come". God, who is all-wise, all-knowing, all-powerful seeks to link his limitless abilities to your limited inabilities; to place his all-mighty power with your insipid powerlessness; to persistently plow through the clods of miscommunication, and thereby furrow a garden, which yields an abundant harvest of love, devotion and faithfulness.

Oh yes, man may be afraid of rejection, but not God. He knows who He is, what He can do and what He will do. He promises to be the solidifying stabilizer in the relationship. He promises to be the provision for our needs, to be the source of our supply, the physician for our surgery and the psychologist when we cry. He can and will do it all, if we will just cooperate. There is no need to fear.

#

THE FIRST LOVE

Dr. Taylor, when answering a woman's question as to why she didn't feel about her husband, the same way she felt, when she first fell in love with him; when there was a "kick-in the stomach" feeling, which made her want to be with him all the time, responded in the following manner:

"The state of being 'in love' can be compared to a hormonal tsunami --that occurs with the brain."

Now a tsunami defined is "a huge sea wave caused by a great disturbance under an ocean, as a strong earthquake or a volcanic eruption." [197]

She went on to say that:

> The anticipation of being with a person to whom you are attracted (usually sexually) can trigger the fight/flight response. Physiologically,

---

[197] Webster's New World College Dictionary - Macmillan, NY, 1996

this is somewhat similar to what you might experience were you being chased by a wild animal! Next, endorphins (the brain's natural morphine) stimulate the release of dopamine (a 'feel good' neurotransmitter). These substances overwhelm the amygdala, part of the brain's inhibition center that wants to introduce a note of caution to be sure you protect yourself... This hormonal tsunami, often called the **honeymoon period,** usually lasts for about 18-24 months. Then the chemistry of attraction begins to wear off and the brain wants to look for something new, different, and more exciting. As the brain gradually becomes accustomed to the relationship, the hormonal tsunami is triggered only periodically. Some individuals get caught up in the initial excitement and seek a new relationship as soon as the 'kick in the stomach' begins to lessen. Consequently, they may never experience the trade-off - that deep, abiding, contented love can grow between committed individuals.[198]

This is a wonderful example of what happens when a person first comes to Christ. Jesus calls it your "first love" [199] In writing to the seven churches of Revelation; Christ had an argument against Ephesus, the very first church. He said:

> I know thy works, and thy labour, and thy patience, and how thou canst not bear them which are evil: and thou hast tried them which say they are apostles, and are not, and hast found them liars: and hast borne, and hast patience, and for my name's sake hast laboured, and hast not fainted. Nevertheless, I have somewhat against thee, because thou hast left thy first love. [200]

---

[198] Dynamic Dialog - Realizations - http://www.arlenetaylor.org/qa/InLove.htm - 2/10/03
[199] Revelation 2:4
[200] ibid 2:2-4

Ephesus constituted the early church, right after Jesus' crucifixion, and his followers shared all of their physical food and belongings, equally among themselves. The church (members) were "on fire" for God preaching everywhere they went; and proclaiming the good news of Jesus Christ, His birth, His death, His resurrection, and the promise of His return. This return would mark the end of the world -- wherein, the wicked are destroyed with the brightness of his coming.[201] Then all the saved, those who sleep in Jesus and those who are alive, when He comes, would be taken to heaven. [202]

There, they would live with Christ and judge the wicked for 1,000 years. At the end of the 1,000 years, the resurrected wicked are destroyed forever. The saints inherit the renewed earth and live in peace eternally.[203] This message was so powerful, until it has lasted down to this time.

---

[201] II Thessalonians 2:8
[202] I Thessalonians 4:16-17
[203] Revelation 20:1-10

However, that first church, Ephesus, grew tired of preaching that message of truth; when they lost their "first love", -- their spiritual tsunami came to an end. They went through that "honeymoon period" Dr. Taylor talks about, and although it lasted far longer than 18-24 months, it did pass over, and the church settled down in complacency, and lost its fire.

Quite often, this is what happens to individual members of the congregation, once they learn to pray. After a while, they do not get the same charge when they pray, as they did at first. Instead of adjusting to a deeper, more committed relationship with God - one that is **not** based on feelings or emotions (right brain), but rather on the facts presented in his word, (left-brain) many seek for something more exciting. Many become deceived this one way, thinking they have received the Holy Spirit, whenever they get excited during a religious service, when it is not the Holy Spirit at all. It is simply their emotions taking over or some other spirit taking control.

Often, they want to "feel" something happening in their physical being, when in actuality the transaction is taking place within the brain. If they could just hold on long enough, the physical change would come. It would come with a sense of release; the tension would begin to drain from the body replaced by a sense of contentment and tranquility.

There is absolutely nothing more exciting than inter-coursing with God. Once you have settled into the comfort of His love; once you have realized the solidity of His promises; once you have grasped the significance of His sacrifice on Calvary, then and only then, can you experience and enjoy the peace He promises to give so abundantly.

# # #

NEVER LET HIM GO

The knowledge which he [Satan], as well as the angels who fell with him, had of the character of God, of His goodness, His mercy, wisdom, and excellent glory, made their guilt unpardonable.

There was no possible hope for those ever to be redeemed, who had witnessed and enjoyed the inexpressible glory of Heaven and had seen the terrible majesty of God, and, in presence of all this glory, had rebelled against Him. There were no new and more wonderful exhibitions of God's exalted power that could ever impress them as deeply as those they had already experienced. **If they could rebel in the very presence of the weight of glory inexpressible, they could not be placed in any more favorable condition to be proved.** There was no reserve force of power, nor were there any greater heights and depths of infinite glory to overpower their jealous doubts and rebellious murmuring. Their guilt and their punishment must be in proportion to their exalted privileges in the heavenly courts.[204]

On the other hand, humanity was fresh and innocent. Although Eve had been deceived into believing the lie Satan had told her, "Ye shall not surely die" [205] and had eaten of the tree of knowledge, yet they were limited in their knowledge and experience of God and of His magnificence. Therefore, upon humankind's fall there lay a way out of their sinful condition; a way up from their fallen state; a way that would link earth to heaven and that way would be via the cross of Calvary.

Jesus would come in all of His divinity; yet He would shroud it in humanity that humankind could be able to bear it.

---
[204]
[205] Genesis 3:7

Then through His perfect life, through His ignominious and vicarious death coupled with His all-powerful resurrection, He could claim the right to salvage man from the junk heap of sin and restore him to perfection.

God would make it impossible for man to say that He could have done more. With Christ He gave all the resources of heaven that nothing might be wanting in the plan for man's uplifting.[206]

The rest is left up to us. Whether you and I are saved or lost is strictly dependent on our choices. We can choose to side with God's enemy (Satan) or we can cast our lot on God's side and declare that we will stand with Him.

There is a 1955 musical, **South Pacific,** which reminds me of God's covenant to His church. In this musical the leading man, a sailor, falls in love with a beautiful woman on an island in the South Seas. He has to leave the island to continue his time with the Navy. However, in the course of all of this, the two of them sing a

---

[206] Australian Union Conference Record, April 1, 1901

song entitled *Some Enchanted Evening*. In this song, two lovers speak of how they met in a crowded room, and immediately they knew the other was his/her true love. Neither one can explain how he or she knows this, but each is determined to rush to that lover's side and abide there forever.

In the last words of the song, you can hear the voice of God singing to His lover (the church) saying, "Once you have found Me, never let Me go, Now that I've found you, I'll ne - ver let, you go!" Those words are God's commitment to you, and they should be your commitment to Him. He is the perfect lover.

God is in love with you, and you are to be in love with Him. Being in love for humans, however, does not mean you will be all over each other constantly, but it does when it comes to God. Jesus says,

If a man love[s] me, he will keep my words: and my Father will love him, and we will come unto him, and make our abode [dwelling] with him"[207]

"I will not leave you comfortless: I will come to you.[208]

When we consider the interactions between human couples, each partner studies the other partner, that he/she might become acquainted with the other's needs, wants and desires. Each partner makes a conscientious decision to allow nothing or anyone to come between him and her. They both are in this relationship for the long haul, good and bad, happy or sad. They are determined to make a future together, to work together, to have children together; to raise them together; to grow old together; and to spend eternity together.

However, when it comes to God, He does not need to study humanity. He made humankind and knows how it works. But you need to study God, through His Word,

---

[207] St. John 14:23
[208] St. John 14:18

so you will know how to please and serve Him; then you will declare like the Psalmist that your "heart is fixed" on God. [209]

This kind of love is what God wants to share with each of us. Once we have given Him our hearts, He says, "Now let's begin to plan our future. In addition, in order to have a good future, we must agree, for 'how can two walk together, unless they agree?' [210] Therefore, we must agree to discuss all decisions with each other before concluding on any action. We must be sure that each action falls within the parameter of our present and/or future plans together before we proceed, because everything we say or do directly affects each other in some way. One of my favorite authors puts it this way:

> As wax retains the figure of the seal, so the mind retains the impression produced by **intercourse** and association. The **influence** may be

---

[209] Psalms 108:1
[210] Amos 3:3

unconscious, yet it is no less powerful."[211]

In order to have a solid future with God, you must allow His influence to overtake you completely. Remember, there is nothing in yourself that can make the relationship work, outside of giving Him your all. For you become His bride by grace, not by works. [212]

> For by grace are ye saved through faith; and that not of yourselves: it is the gift of God: Not of works, lest any man should boast." "Therefore, by the deeds of the law there shall no flesh be justified in his sight: ...[213]

You are only able to stay faithful to Him, because of His promise to:

---

[211] Ellen White - The **OFFICIAL** Ellen G. White Website – Devotional, To Have Friends We Must Be Friendly
[212] Ephesians 2:8-9
[213] Romans 3:20

... put my law in their [your] inward parts, and write it in their [your] hearts; and will be their [your] God, and they [you] shall be my people."[214]

By complying with these scriptures, you will take pleasure in your "first love" experience; your intercourse will happen more frequently, and prove to be more satisfying. You will learn to "Pray without ceasing"[215] and move effortlessly into that deep abiding love and tranquility God seeks to share with you. Moreover, once you have truly found Him, you will **"NEVER LET HIM GO!"**

###

---

[214] Jeremiah 31:33
[215] I Thessalonians 5:17

OTHER BOOKS AVAILABLE

- Prayer: Intimacy With God
    - Prayer: Intimacy With God Workbook
- The Simplification of the Biblical Sanctuary
- How-To Deal With Adversity
- My Bible Reader Book I
- The Care Free Bears
- The Joy of Motherhood

CONTACT INFORMATION

Twitter - http://bit.ly/Gingertwit

Pinterest - http://bit.ly/GingerPin

Google+ - http://bit.ly/Gingergoogle

LinkedIn - http://bit.ly/Gingerlinkedin

Articulate Com Website -

http://bit.ly/1WQJ1hB

Quotes Rain - http://bit.ly/GingerQuote

Amazon - http://bit.ly/GingerAmazon

Free on Amazon 27/28 -

http://bit.ly/Gingerfree

All Books on

Amazon http://amzn.to/1VPgSIP

PRAYER: INTIMACY WITH GOD

Prayer: Intimacy with God is a highly spiritual and scripturally well-documented exchange regarding God's intent toward His children when they pray.

It delightfully defines the sexual phraseology used freely by God toward His bride, the church. It clarifies the intimacy expected by God, when one approaches Him in prayer, if one truly expects serenity. One can only become intimate with another to the extent that one is willing to be vulnerable with the other.

It is a "must read" for anyone wishing to experience a deeper, more powerful prayer relationship with God.

"When we know God as it is our privilege to know Him, our life will be a life of continual obedience. Through an appreciation of the character of Christ, through communion with God, sin will become hateful to us."

E. G. White – Desire of Ages – 'Let Not Your Heart Be Troubled' p.668, Pacific Press, Mountain View, CA

ABOUT THE AUTHOR

Virginia is the sole proprietor of Articulate Communications, a multi-faceted business, which includes desktop publishing, business writing, workshop presentations and keynote speaking.

Additionally, she is a lay-evangelistic preacher of the gospel, prison ministry volunteer, prayer warrior, former college professor and radio show host.

She is married to John H. Harrison and lives in Bristow, OK

www.ingramcontent.com/pod-product-compliance
Lightning Source LLC
Chambersburg PA
CBHW061637040426
42446CB00010B/1456